AUTUMN LEAVES

Autumn Leaves

by

ANDRÉ GIDE

Translated from the French
"FEUILLETS D'AUTOMNE"
by
ELSIE PELL

PHILOSOPHICAL LIBRARY
New York

15 EAST 40TH STREET
NEW YORK CITY, N. Y.

ISBN 978-0-8065-3046-4

PRINTED IN THE UNITED STATES OF AMERICA

CONTENTS

PAGE

1

SPRING

IN my time (I mean at the time of my youth), it did not happen this way.

We would not have put up with these false exits, these re-entrances, these unexpected returns of winter after the stage was already set for the new fantasy. In my time, they knew how to abide by the rules. Rimbaud could write: "Eucharis tells me it is spring"; and after that you didn't have to light the stoves any more. And it is not so much that the actors don't know their roles to-day, but that they play them unseasonably. For ten or fifteen years springtime's entrance has been a wash-out. You would like to go to the opening performance; nothing is ready. A glacial wind whistles through the delicate frondescence; the fruit-trees have budded too soon; they wait in vain for heaven's answer and warm breezes; the bees are numb and fertilization jeopardized; you say: it is postponed until later, and you bury yourself again in meditation and reading; but no: the play has begun just the same; and when, on raising your eyes from the book, you look out, you are distressed to see that the impatient vegetation is going right along without worrying too much because the rest of the orchestra is lagging behind or is not following.

In my time, winter tiptoed away; step by step, it gave up its place; it had finally pronounced its last word, and you counted on the sun; the sap could mount without fear and the swollen buds open. Even then we would have been willing for spring to be late; but not for it to beat about the bush and to lose its ease and grace in those altercations with the bad season, up to the point of becoming unrecognizable; with the result that (I know exactly what's going to happen), again this year, summer is going to arrive suddenly as though it came immediately after winter.

At least, this year, before meeting up again with the north wind and the gloom of the sky in Paris, I had left behind, half hidden under the flowers, the beautiful ruins of Olympus. Leaving Greece regretfully, I had passed through Yugoslavia fallen a prey to a frenzy of pink and white, admired the groves of wild lilac, fruit-trees, cherry or pear, quivering with whiteness, and here and there the slender, rosy sprays of peach-trees, all more beautiful than I remembered they could be; then, at the edge of the water, a great yellow flower, with the bearing of the asphodel, that I was not yet acquainted with, and whose name I should have liked to know.

The image of spring is formed by the superimpression of many memories. To those of former days are now added for me that of the marvelous public gardens of Athens; an avenue of Judas-trees forming an arch, a vast space completely covered by fragrant bunches of wistaria, where, on numerous benches, an entire nation, idle, came to listen to the singing of the birds, and to forget, for an hour, the occupation of Albania.

I don't remember being very sensitive to spring in my early youth. I think the small child for whom everything is new, is not very surprised at miracles. The springtime of life begins with adolescence. When the heart swells with a vague love and virtuous resolutions at the same time, and the flesh with restless desires, then only one understands, by feeling it in the same way within oneself, the miraculous springtide. Yes, to be sensitive to spring, collusion is necessary and one must take part in the game itself. Then the adolescent suddenly trembles on hearing, at dawn, the song of the blackbird (rue de Commaille, where I then lived with my mother; the window of my room opened on a deep garden) ; he blushes on hearing his throbbing secret divulged; then cheers up; the whole city is still sleeping; he is the only one to hear; it is a matter between the blackbird and himself; and when man in his turn awakes, the bird falls silent.

(A little later I spent my Easter vacation in Calvados. . . .) Anyone who has not gotten up before dawn does not know all the quivering, the uncertain rustling, the murmuring, that can glide into the copses in the springtime. The ardent adolescent, tormented by an unknown restlessness, leaves his scorching bed to go in quest of the key to the mystery. It is the hour when the sky, in the east, begins to pale. Like a prisoner escaping, he leaves his room, goes groping along the corridor still in darkness; he descends the stairs noiselessly, carefully avoiding the step which he knows his foot would make creak, for he is afraid of waking his mother; he draws the bolts of the streetdoor, which he opens; and now he is under the vast sky, alone, wild with delight and skipping like a dancer; his step, as he crosses the yard, is so light that it hardly makes the gravel crunch; he runs toward the footpath in the woods, enters it, offers his face to the dew that the branches are shaking on it; he is in league with the game; the deer do not flee; the squirrel hides behind a tree but it is for the fun of it; he comes to the edge of the wood and, on the damp fields, surprises the erotic gambols of the hare and his doe. When, intoxicated with delight and rapture, he reaches home where his parents are still asleep, he hears sounding afar off the angelus.

I have seen, since, the plains of Morocco turn iridescent, become sprinkled with orange-colored marigolds, with little blue convolvulus and with many a smiling flower. I have seen, under the palm trees of El Kantara, sheltered by the high palms, the white apricot-trees which, humming with bees, shelter in turn the barley fields. I have seen the cemetery of Blidah (which is now, alas! nothing but a barracks) fill up with roses; its sacred woods with the singing of birds. I came there as a convalescent and felt, as though within me, the whole of nature finally awakening from her winter lethargy. I have seen the plains of Lombardy risk their first smiles; I have seen Rome and Florence filling up with bouquets. . . .

Some years ago, I wanted to surprise, on the icy plateaus of the Alps, the first quivering of life in answer to the first caresses of the sun. But I got there too soon; on the close-cropped turf the melting of the snow made little lakes in which were reflected the austere pines and the skeleton-like larch-trees. Some russet heather seemed to be resigned to death; nothing was ready; nature was still sulking. I thought I was on the boards of a theatre during the intermission, when they are getting ready for a change of scenery; I was indiscreetly present at what the drop-curtain hides from the eyes of the audience awaiting the striking of the gong; and it might also have been said that, half dried of winter, there still trailed over the ground, as in a room during the process of moving, rotten matting and those hideous cloths used for scouring the flagstones and that are called, I believe, *serpillières,* of which the mounds of rusty, old, last year's ferns made me think irresistibly. And I was about to turn back toward more pleasing country, when suddenly, on climbing up a little eminence and leaving behind me the sleeping forest, I discovered, on an open space where patches of snow still lingered, a mass of little white crocuses, silky and delicate, that could no longer restrain their impatience to put in a word, and were risking their fragility through the thick carpet of the mosses. And I could have wept for tenderness, for this reaffirmation of love and life never seems more moving than when death surrounds it. In like manner the big pale lavender choke-weeds took on an unexpected elegance in the desolate sand of the desert. So it was at Olympus, that last spring among the ruins.

I remember . . . it was beyond Touggourt; we had ridden for a long time over the arid dunes to reach a miserable village composed of a few low sand-colored houses; insensible to the seasons, it appeared. The few Arabs parked there, around a Zaouia, must have partaken of life in a very sorry fashion; anchorites, doubtless, who had no contacts except with God. One of the monks led us into a little inner courtyard, without shade or coolness, but in the middle of which diligent care was keeping alive a very delicate bush that the season was inviting, in spite of the barrenness all around, to bloom. I remember the tender smile of the Arab when, indicating to us his few fragrant flowers, he said only: Yasmin! and our eyes filled with tears.

Yes, it is of all those memories piled one on the other that I construct the abstract image of spring. And that, too, is what causes my restlessness on the first fine days: I should like to be able to contemplate the springtide everywhere at the same time. With the result that I am not perfectly comfortable anywhere, even if it were in the most beautiful garden in the world, or even in my little garden at Cuverville at the time when I was personally acquainted with each flower. As soon as the air is warm enough and the sky blue, I wish to evaporate into the whole of nature, carried away by the passing breeze, floating without bonds here and there. Oh! never to be anywhere but somewhere! never to be anyone but someone. . . .

* * *

Springtime is a gradual growth; it is the season of preparation and of hope. I have always preferred the bud full of promise to the full bloom of the flower, desire to possession, progress to achievement, adolescence to maturity. Not that there is any disappointment in summer, but it is a season at its zenith which will end in decline. "Summer is the season of nest building," said Victor Hugo; "spring, the season of love." If the flower were not attached to its stem, it would flee at the approach of man, like the insect or the bird; for the attribute of man on the earth, at least as long as he does not better understand his role, is to worry and frighten what he is not interested in taming for utilitarian purposes. Man is skillful in mistreating everything he can use; often skillful equally, alas! for material reasons, in putting a check, all about him, on happiness. The gardens he arranges are beautiful, but could be very much more so. Most of the time, he confuses, messes up and breaks the harmony. If his ingenuity concerned itself with protecting the rare and exquisite which is almost always the delicate and weak, if he took greater care to favor the joy of others than to sacrifice it in order to entrench his own authority more firmly, "the face of the world" could be changed.

But this impulse toward blissfulness that each springtime introduces to us remains as delusive as the full bloom of summer. We see only the elect, who are but a very small number compared to the enormous number of the failures, the eliminated, of those who do not attain happiness. Darwin gives a striking picture of that field of battle that is the tiniest patch of earth where everything that lives enters necessarily into competition and struggles ferociously, desperately for life, struggles for pleasure and for love. In the vegetable world, the strongest and best endowed supplant and strangle the weak, rob them of their nourishing sap, the air, the place that their need of joy would have the right to expect. Unless we bend over them, we do not see the latter, but only those that triumph; and if the whole earth, in the springtime, seems to offer us an immense hymn of joy, it is because we remain deaf to the *Vae Victis*. Already on a single plant, on the same tree, how many sleeping shoots will never awaken to life! How many buds will remain unopened, how many flowers unfertilized, or whose efforts will afterwards remain vain to profit by a sufficiency of sap that their neighbors, more greedy or better placed, will steal from them. It happens that the gardener lends an expert hand to these dramas in our orchards and gardens; in order to obtain a larger flower, a heavier fruit, he suppresses with authority twin promises.

In the animal kingdom, we gaze at the happy couples; the rejected and the bruised hide away. For certain species we know that one insect out of a hundred arrives at fulfillment; for others, one out of a thousand. Sometimes a single male jealously reserves his personal rights over a whole seraglio; woe to the other males who approach it or woe to him. And from species to species, even if one does not sacrifice the other to his own subsistence, murderous rivalries maintain a sort of equilibrium disputed ceaselessly, in the perpetual competition for space and nourishment. The appearance of happiness is obtained only by the almost immediate elimination of the infirm and the weak. Nature acts like those South Sea Islanders who, we are told, make the sick and the aged climb up into a tree, on certain holidays, then shake the tree and sacrifice those who have not the strength to hold on. After which the traveler who comes up can admire, you can bet on it! the smiling and jolly aspect of the population.

Most certainly it would be imprudent to draw from these statements any teaching whatever. Moreover it is not as a moralist that I speak here. I am not of those who search and find lessons endlessly, and everywhere, without for that reason becoming any wiser. Nor am I of those who say:

I dream of summers that last
Forever

and I believe it preferable to adapt oneself as well as possible to what is. I find charm and pleasure in alternation, rather than in continuity. The perpetual summer of the tropics is vexing in that it prevents the springtime. As Saint-Amant said so exquisitely:

The orange on the same day ripens and buds,
And during all the months can be seen in those
places
Both spring and summer blending in with the
autumn . . .

so that one never knows where one is. I like the seasons well defined, and see to it that I do not confuse the kinds. Among the flowers, I forget the fruits, and reserve the ratiocinations for winter.

2

YOUTH

LAST year, while visiting Jean Schlumberger who was my neighbor in the country, at the time that I was "a man of property" in Calvados, I went back to see La Roque where, as I relate elsewhere, I spent so long a time pleasantly in my childhood. The property is now completely enclosed by barbed wire. On seeing it I feel within me the soul of a communist. I never had a possessive one. The very word property owner seems to me ridiculous and odious. As for this estate, that I inherited from my mother when I was still very young, I suffered at knowing the exact extent of its boundaries; or rather, I would not allow myself to know them; not so that I could imagine I owned more, but, on the contrary, to keep myself from thinking that any of all this that I loved here was personally and exclusively *my* property. When, in the evening, I seated myself on the other side of the hill from which the wooded country becomes visible, the grassy foot-hills, the clumps of trees, the brushwood, the course of the little river often hidden by the high willow-herbs, the alders and the hazel-trees, could very well cease to be mine without losing their attraction for all that. I remained contemplative and did not feel any more obligations toward the country than the country felt for me.

In 1896, the news that Robidet came to announce to me triumphantly on a certain fine holiday, fell on me like a catastrophe. Thanks to his zealous machinations, I had just been elected mayor. He had been maneuvering that for a long time; without my knowledge, needless to say. But first it was necessary to wait until I had reached the legal age and until the mayor whom I should succeed had given up the position. He died just as I was entering my twenty-fifth year. Robidet, who already held the double duties of keeper and factor, was still intriguing to obtain those of deputy mayor, to which the great service he was thus rendering the community and his master, designated him naturally. He was counting on my lack of taste for authority, and thought very pertinently that my easy going nature and my youth would assure him absolute power. Robidet, who was already reigning during my mother's lifetime and whom I had inherited from her along with the property, thought little, talked a great deal, and sized up everyone according to himself. His conduct was solely guided by self-interest and respect for convention. "Oh! sir, that isn't done," he said to me, when I wanted to have a cripple who was making his way painfully along the road get into the cariole that was taking us to the market at Lisieux; and, to get by him more quickly, a cut from the whip put the horse to a gallop. He was, moreover, of a very questionable honesty, but safeguarded appearances and was skillful in taking refuge behind "custom," as soon as it happened that I wanted to examine his accounts. He seemed to get into the good graces of everyone at my expense. That is what may explain that the six farms and the woods that comprised the estate of La Roque, spread over several communes, never brought me in anything but worries.

I was newly married. I was walking, I remember, in an avenue of the garden, between my wife and my friend Eugène Rouart who, entirely devoted to politics and as up-to-date as I was not, straightway expounded to me the advantages this election offered me. From the town hall to council general there was only a step; another to the Chamber of Deputies. My career was marked out. And Robidet, who was surprised at the reddening of my countenance, approved it. Em said nothing, understanding better the reasons for my sudden gloom; entire nature around me lost its enchantment. Complicated relationships of the practical order would oppose themselves henceforth to the disinterestedness of my glances.

My love affairs with the country would cease to be platonic. I felt myself already beleaguered by the crushing care of new duties. It would be the end of dreams and contemplative walks. Nevertheless Em herself considered that I could not decline. It was in the interest of everyone, she maintained. For she was well enough acquainted with me to know that, once I was mayor, I would not be willing to be so half-heartedly, since I took nothing lightly. So I accepted. And those who claim that I am indifferent to public affairs surely cannot imagine the civic zeal that I observed in the exercise of my very absorbing functions.

One of my first acts was to have an alcoholic interned in the sanitarium of Bon-Sauveur at Caen. Alcohol was surreptitiously consuming the country; and very much more than statistics let it be known, for they took account only of official consumption in the officially licensed liquor stores. But along with that, were the uncontrolled clandestine sales by all the home-distiller farmers. Since the factories daily skimmed the countryside, making private dairies useless, even the women drank much more. Everyone living in my commune was more or less alcoholic. Compared with those farmers of robust appearance, some of them of colossal stature, my rather delicate appearance made a very poor example of my sobriety. But I can congratulate myself on one cure in the person of Goret, the husband of the woman interned. As I was accompanying him to Caen where he was going to see his wife again, once more a prey to *delirium tremens,* I took it upon myself to frighten him. I made him stick out his tongue, I turned back his lips and his eye-lids, with a very competent air, examining his reflexes and the bending back of his thumb which I declared characteristic and very disquieting. "My poor friend," I ended by declaring in a learned tone, while Robidet who was driving the cariole jeered to reassure him, "you haven't three months before joining your wife. Perhaps less, if you do not stop tomorrow." At first Robidet shrugged his shoulders, but afterwards he told me that, since that day, Goret had completely reformed.

Robidet rendered me his best service by always pointing out again each one of the men under my supervision. He knew only too well the weakness that, all my life, has played me absurd tricks and made me commit the most unfortunate breaks: not to be able to recognize people. That accounts for the uncertainty in my approach, which has often been taken for haughtiness, disdain or indifference; for anyone you do not recognize is not easily persuaded, even after being warned, that the lack of recognition is sincere. The people under my direction were, thank goodness, not numerous. As though to try my strength, France had reserved for her youngest mayor one of her tiniest communes. And the small number of its inhabitants continued to diminish, the mortality rate gaining each year over the births. While I now inhabit one of the most prolific regions in France, and, in order to present a family for the Cognacq legacy, I would be embarrassed only by the choice, the homes at La Roque were, for the greater part, childless. You must not picture a village; not even a little group of houses around a church. Scattered over the land, nothing but farms, often more than a kilometer apart. But not one was more isolated than that of Pierre B., my youngest farmer, son of the deceased mayor whom I succeeded. Pierre had recently taken as his wife one of the nicest girls in the region. A servant of fourteen or fifteen years of age, sister of the wife, lived with the newly wed couple; the latter, for a wonder, was pregnant; so I was particularly interested in this couple.

Madame Pierre B. was close to confinement when bad luck would have it that her husband was called away to a rather distant market where he was to buy some cattle. Two days of absence only; business first.

Pierre B. had no sooner left, than his wife's labor began.

"I have an idea it is not going to be easy," the young woman said to her sister. "It hurts a great deal, but I don't think it is going as it should. How beastly that Pierre is gone."

Then a little later:

"Perhaps it would be better just the same if you went to get the doctor at Lisieux. Pierre could not find any fault with that. Don't be afraid to leave me alone. I still have a little time."

Lisieux is twelve kilometers away. The child runs there. The doctor who is only a young supply, brings her back in his two wheeled carriage (there were not any autos yet). Not very well informed by the child who is a little stupid, he does not bring with him any of the instruments needed in case of a difficult delivery. Besides he is not a surgeon. He has hurried, it is true, and the child has run fast; but three hours have passed since she left her sister. When the doctor arrives, night is falling. . . .

When Pierre B. returned the next morning from market, he could see from the doorway, for the bedroom door had been left open, an abominable sight. On the unmade bed covered with blood, his lifeless young wife, her abdomen wide open. At the foot of the bed, a bundle of gory flesh: all that remained of the child. In the room frightful disorder; on the floor and on the table, bloody instruments: a knife, a cleaver, a skewer. As the forceps were not sufficient, kitchen utensils coming to his aid, told of the panic of the too young doctor, alone in that badly lighted room, losing his head and asking help of everything he could lay his hands on. The terrified servant had taken flight at the beginning of the operation.

My indignation was unlimited. I made up my mind to go find the doctor: to start a case against him. I had myself driven to Lisieux, but stopped the carriage before the door. I got out; I can still see the spot. I recall the street and the house. I see myself again taking a hundred steps, preparing my charge, and trying to imagine the disconcerted being before whom I was going to find myself; that young doctor, whose career I was going to break, was doubtless no eagle, but a boy almost as young as I was, inexperienced, who would tell me that, in the frightful combination of circumstances, all the experience in the world would not have made up for the total lack of means of help. Tramping up and down, I imagined his anguish, his groping in the dark, his panic, his despair, and I relived that nightmare so well that finally I went back to the carriage, no longer having the heart to crush the unhappy man more.

I applied more perseverance in the Mulot affair. I wrote the preceding only so as to come finally to Mulot. Ah! that one, I would have recognized him anywhere. He would have been enough to make me love the country. I become attached to a region really through its people. I was finding in my commune only petty interests, rapacity, slyness, all the elementary forms of selfishness; only wooden countenances, cunning or glum; only uncouth or deformed bodies. Mulot was not from that part of the country. A Norman however, but not like any other, and of such distinction in his manners that I could easily have imagined him the illegitimate son of some lord. And on certain days, I preferred to imagine him of Russian blood, so as to explain to myself the affectionate gentleness of his look of a moujik. He wore mutton-chop whiskers like the people of Calvados. He was not handsome, to be sure; but his facial features were not common or set, nothing cheap about them. Above all, he expressed himself with much more purity than anyone in my commune. He was a little more than forty years of age when I became mayor and began to notice him. I immediately conceived an unusual affection for him. I never met him without speaking to him and often I went out of my way to go see him work. A simple laborer, an "odd-job man," Robidet employed him for the heaviest jobs. The laying and upkeep of drains was one of his specialties. Robidet had persuaded my mother to drain several sloping fields where the water ran off badly because of the nature of the soil, and where the grass gave way to rush sedge, horse-tail and reeds. When badly laid, too close to the level of the earth, or too narrow, the pipes of the drains were quickly invaded by the roots of some subterranean vegetation or other, hairy, matted roots that stopped them up. To counteract this, long rods of metal were inserted into the pipes; but they soon struck against an obstacle; and if you kept on, the pipe broke. Then the ground had to be opened, the drains detached, taken up, unstopped or replaced. This work took days. Every six months it had all to be done over again. It was dear and did not improve the field any, but interested me particularly, for I was trying to find out what plants could produce such over-developed roots, which Mulot was bringing out in enormous wads. I recall him bending over the spongy earth, his face half hidden by the rushes, wet, covered with mud, pushing the metal rod. . . .

"Do you see this drainage, sir? It's of no use to you or the field. And it has to be repaired all the time. The cattle, on passing over it, pull apart the joints and break the pipes. Out of ten, six have to be replaced. You can't help thinking that those who ordered the work (he did not mention Robidet by name) found it to their advantage. . . ."

Besides he never complained at all, but kept saying:

"If I work like this, it is so that my children can follow another trade."

Mulot had two sons and three daughters. The eldest son, a husky fellow of sixteen years, worked at the blacksmith shop on the square; he had progressive ideas, did not associate with the country people, and ran over to Lisieux for his companions as soon as he had a free day. If I got a bow from him when I passed, that was all.

"Yes," said Mulot, "he is proud. It embarrasses him to speak to anyone who knows what his father does. Yet it isn't because he looks down on me. . . . Well, when it comes to your children, you can't always do what you want with them. At least the others give me only pleasure."

Mulot lived with them all in an old mill, below the pond which, formerly, fed the waterfall. The paddle-wheel that could still be seen at the side of the house, had been out of use for a long time. The house was clean and neat. A young woman kept house. Her age would not let you take her for the mother of Mulot's children. There was a real Madame Mulot some place all right; nobody knew where; how long since she had left. . . . After many proceedings and much trouble, Mulot had just obtained the divorce.

"I never had any luck," he said to me. "But the worst that ever happened to me I owe to that woman. Listen, Monsieur Gide, she knew how much I loved my children. When she left, she took them all with her. On purpose to hurt me; for she cared practically nothing for them. She lived several months not far from here with a country bumpkin who had just come into money and could offer the little ones more comfort than they could find here. I was going to appeal to the law to get them back. And then, one evening, on returning from work, there were the five kiddies waiting for me at home. I could only think that the other one had had enough of them. . . . They had come back on foot, the oldest boy carrying the baby girl. They said they had been sent away. And in such a state, Monsieur Gide! They had almost nothing on their bodies, but their heads full of lice, and thin, and filthy! . . . I could have cried for sorrow as much as for joy at seeing them. . . . Look! You see those roots? I have a notion it's horse-tail."

And he handed me a matted wad he had just taken out of the drain. Then he went on:

"Monsieur knows I am going to get married again?"

"No, Mulot, nobody told me anything about it."

"I was waiting to get the divorce. Oh! it is someone that the children know very well. She is like a big sister to them; and gentle and neat. . . ."

"Well, Mulot, I am not mayor for nothing. Whenever you wish."

Some time after, I assumed my sash of honor for the first time for the purpose of uniting the new couple. The ceremony took place exactly on the anniversary date of my own marriage; in addition to my attachment for Mulot, that did not fail to move me, and I was preparing to make a discreet allusion to it, but Robidet said:

"Above all, Monsieur must not make a speech. They are people who don't deserve it. You must marry them quickly without saying anything to them."

The commune is so small that it did not have, properly speaking, a city-hall. The general living-room of one of the farms, at the edge of the road, near the little church, was used instead. On occasion, the farmer served as restaurant keeper, and each meeting of the council was followed by a copious repast from which everybody went out flushed and not too steady on his legs. The farmer's wife was a wonderful cook. Paul Fort and Ghéon whom I invited to one of those reunions, at a time when they were my guests at La Roque[1], doubtless remember a certain creamed veal. . . . They remember, too, the passing of little glasses, filled turn about with rum, fine champagne and apple-brandy, preceded moreover by libations of thick, dark cider, more heady than the most generous of wines. And suddenly one of the members of the council got up, rolled on the floor, and writhed in the atrocious pains of an ulcerated stomach. . . .

[1] Ghéon had just finished *Le Pain;* Paul Fort, *Louis XI;* I, my *Saül;* and we had met to read them to each other.

I return to Mulot. Not being able to content myself with seeing him kept down to such inferior tasks, I had gotten it into my head to appoint him keeper, replacing Cherhomme, a perfect rogue who fleeced me, trading on his hunting and that of the poachers with whom he stood in well. I opened my heart to Robidet.

"You have to be sworn in to be keeper. Mulot can not, due to his police record."

"Mulot has been sentenced?"

"Monsieur did not know it?"

"But sentenced for what?"

"Monsieur has only to ask him if he wishes to know."

The same evening I went to find Mulot who was working near the lime kiln. He was at the bottom of a big hole that he was digging still deeper with a pick and shovel. I drew near the edge and leaned over like Hamlet in his dialogue with the grave-digger.

"Ah, they told you," he said, somewhat embarrassed at first, raising his faithful, dog-like eyes to me.

"No, Mulot, I don't know anything. Only one thing, that you were sentenced to prison. But why? . . ."

He seemed to hesitate; shrugged his shoulders, then:

"You want me to tell you the story, sir?"

(Of all the people in my commune, Mulot was the only one who did not speak to me in the third person.)

"I came to listen to you," I said to him.

But he didn't begin his story at once. First he said:

"Oh! I was cut out for better things. . . . I am educated, Monsieur Gide."

And all this in such a tone of voice that the tears came to my eyes.

"What do you expect! That filthy affair has always prevented me from going higher. I hoped to become factor in the Orne where I lived before coming here. Yes, factor. That suited me fine. The property was considerable. To make it pay, they needed a manager. I presented myself at the chateau. It was a lady who lived in it. You perhaps know. . . . (And he told me a name that I heard for the first time.) Naturally I showed her my papers; I had very good references from my employers. Madame X told me that I pleased her. The affair was practically concluded and I had only to come back. If you only knew how happy I was! When I arrived on the appointed day, Madame could not receive me. She had looked me up, of course! . . . No, Monsieur, you see, with a police record, you can expect nothing. Since then, I haven't tried any more. I came here. Now you see my work. Oh! I don't tell you all this to complain. But . . . I would like something else for my children."

He began to dig again, dropping his head and wanting also, it seemed to me, to hide his tears.

"So, Mulot, you don't want to tell me why you were sentenced?"

"Oh! Monsieur Gide, don't think that. It's true I don't like to talk about it. But I can very well tell you the story. I was still young. I was returning from my military service. My parents didn't have much money and I had to earn my living. I accepted work with an older brother, as digger for the Western Railroad Company. They took us on with several others to raise an embankment that was collapsing on the Paris-Havre line. It was not exactly an embankment but a steep incline with grass and bushes. . . . All that went on during the hunting season. You could hear the gun-shots. The hunters couldn't be far away. But the land along the road belongs to the Company. You know, sir, there are wire fences all along to keep people out. So when we saw a hare coming, we said to each other that he knew that, too, and that he was coming to protect himself. But the hunters who were chasing him brought him down all the same. And then they passed over the wires to come pick him up. Naturally, we wouldn't have said anything. But on the opposite bank there were two policemen who ran after them to make out their report. What do you expect? They were doing their duty, those men. . . . The hunters began to get mad and, as they were already far away from the bank with their hare, they defied the police to prove that the hare had been shot on the track. Then the police, who knew we had seen everything, had me, my brother, and also three others summoned as witnesses. The affair became complicated because those gentlemen had jeered at the police and refused to pay the fine. That made quite a case which could have turned out badly for them. But out of those four hunters, there was one who was a deputy's son, another, nephew of one of the members of the Company. So the witnesses got scared. Perhaps they got something else too, to keep quiet, something that I refused. . . . I can't prove anything. . . . All that I know is that, when they were summoned, they all backed down. They said they hadn't seen anything. But I couldn't say I hadn't seen anything when the hare came to die at my feet."

"So?"

"So they acquitted the hunters."

"But, Mulot, that doesn't tell me why you were convicted, you who hadn't done anything."

"Why, of course, for false witness. The only one to tell the truth is the one who becomes the liar."

I was so astonished I couldn't find anything to say. Mulot gave a few blows with his pick, then:

"Now, look, Monsieur Gide, what hurt me the most in all this story, is to have been let down by my brother. He had seen everything the same as I had. He must have understood very well that, by his denying everything like the others, it was I who would be sentenced."

Mulot had pronounced the last words in a pathetic tone that was not usual for him. But he lowered his voice almost immediately, and it was with a sort of gentleness that he added:

"False witness! . . . I understand that, for a keeper or factor, you prefer something else. Well, what is there to do about it?"

A terrible indignation rushed over me like a sort of mystical aura.

"But, Mulot, that's monstrous. We must. . . . We must be able. . . ."

"You can't do anything, Monsieur Gide. Believe me. At the time, I had hard work accepting it. It's hard, you understand, to be sentenced for something you didn't do. . . . But I was helpless. I had to give in. The matter was settled. I served my sentence. Two years of prison. Afterwards, I moved away. Now I don't think of it any more. I try not to think of it any more."

And he began to dig again.

I left him with a heavy heart. I was at the age when injustice causes unbearable misery. (Oh! I haven't grown up very much on that score.) I neither wanted to, nor could I make up my mind to accept that sentence of Mulot's. Toward the end of my vacation, I saw Mulot again.

"I'm going back to Paris soon," I said to him, "and I. . . ."

"Don't do anything, sir. Believe me. It's useless."

But as soon as I got back to town, I looked around among my acquaintances for someone who could give me good advice, inform me as to the steps I should take to procure the rehabilitation of Mulot. I knew my classmate, Léon Blum, then just a simple "auditeur" in the Conseil d'Etat, was well versed in law. It was he whom I went to consult. He informed me, to my childish astonishment, that an appeal for pardon could not be obtained without a complete review of the case. What an affair! Find all the original witnesses again; subpoena them once more; make the acquitted appear, those people who had become important, and to whom the acquittal of Mulot would bring a retrospective sentence. . . . I would do better to give up.

* * * *

Time passed. I had sold La Roque: part of the farms to Charles Mérouvel, the illustrious author of *Chaste et flétrie;* then the rest to a M. M. . . . who soon resold it to the Count Hély d'Oissel. Nothing called me back to that part of the country but my old friendship for my former neighbor in the country. During a visit in his home, ten or fifteen years after the sale, I again saw Robidet who was still living in the neighborhood. He had bought a house from Mérouvel along the highway opposite the blacksmith-shop.

"Perhaps Monsieur remembers Mulot?" he asked me, in the course of a boring and endless conversation, for the years had not made him less talkative. "Well, he has become mayor of X." (It was a little neighboring commune.)

"And his police record?"

"Outlawed by the statute of limitations."

"I am very happy for his sake."

"Oh! he wasn't such a bad fellow, in spite of that matter of morals."

"That matter of morals?"

"Why his sentence!"

"What are you talking about? Mulot was sentenced for false testimony. Unjustly besides."

Then Robidet mockingly:

"Umph! For rape of a little girl. . . . It's true, at that time, we didn't dare tell Monsieur."

3

MY MOTHER

I

WHEN I had finished my first studies, my mother thought it would be a good thing to introduce me to "society". But aside from some not too distant cousins and the wives of a few of my father's colleagues at the Faculty of Law, transplanted from Rouen to Paris, she had never tried to make any acquaintances. Furthermore, the world in which it seemed I was to be interested, that of men of letters or artists, was not "her" world; she would have felt herself out of place in it.

I no longer know to what drawing-room she took me that day. It must have been that of my cousin Saussine, at whose home, on the rue d'Athènes, I took tiresome dancing lessons twice a week. It was the day they received. There were numerous introductions, and the conversation was approximately what all society conversations are, made up of little nothings and affectations. I turned my attention less to the other ladies than to my mother. I scarcely recognized her. She, ordinarily so modest, so reserved, and seemingly fearful of her own opinion, appeared in that social gathering, full of assurance and, without pushing herself forward at all, perfectly at her ease. One would have said that she was playing a role exactly as it should be, without, moreover, attaching any importance to it, but willingly consenting to mingle in the game of the society parade to which one contributes hardly anything but outward appearances. It even seemed to me that, in the twaddle and foolishness all about, a few particularly sensible sentences of hers, threw the general conversation into disorder; the ridiculous remarks immediately collapsed and disappeared into thin air, like ghosts at the crowing of the cock. I was amazed, and told her so, as soon as we escaped from that Vanity Fair, and found ourselves alone together.

For my part, I dined that evening with Pierre Louys, I believe. At any rate, I remember that I left her as we turned the corner of rue d'Athènes. But I came back to her almost immediately after dinner. I was in a hurry to see her. We were then living on the rue de Commaille. The windows of our apartment opened on a deep garden that no longer exists to-day. My mother was on the balcony. She had taken off her finery, and I rediscovered her in her simple, drab, everyday clothes. It was the season when the first acacias smell sweet. My mother seemed worried;

she did not make confidences easily and doubtless the co-operation of springtime was needed to invite her to speak.

"Is what you said to me as we left our cousin's true?" she began with a great effort. "You really think so? I was . . . well, as good as the others?"

And as I began to exclaim, she continued mournfully:

"If your father had told me so even once . . . I never dared ask him, and I needed so terribly to know, when we went out together, if he was . . ."

She was silent for a moment. I looked at her trying to hold back her tears. She finished in a lower tone of voice, hardly audible:

". . . if he was pleased with me."

I think that those were her exact words which suddenly let me understand how many worries, unasked questions and expectations could, under the appearance of happiness, still dwell in even the most united of couples. And such were my parents in the eyes of everyone and of their son. What my mother had vainly awaited was not a compliment from my father, but only the assurance that she had been able to prove herself worthy of him, that he had not been disappointed in her. But what my father thought, I knew no more than she; and I understood, that evening, that every soul carries to the tomb to hide it there, some secret.

MY MOTHER

II

Everything that was natural in my mother, I loved. But it happened that her impulses were checked by convention and the bent that a bourgeois education too often leaves behind it. (Not always; thus I remember that she dared brave the disapproval of all her family when she went to care for the farmers of La Roque attacked during a typhus epidemic.) That education, excellent, doubtless, when it is a question of curbing evil instincts, attacks equally, but then very unfortunately, the generous emotions of the heart; then a sort of calculation restrains or directs them. I should like to give an example of this:

My mother announced to me her intention of making a gift of Littré to Anna Shackelton, our poor friend, whom I loved as a son. I was bursting with joy, when she added:

"The one I gave your father is bound in morocco. I thought that, for Anna, a shagreen binding would be sufficient."

I understood at once, what I had not known before, that shagreen costs much less. The joy suddenly left my heart. And without a doubt my mother noticed it, for she went on quickly:

"She won't see the difference."

No, that shabby cheating was not natural to her.

To her, giving was natural. But I was irritated also by that sort of complicity to which she invited me.

I have lost the memory of a thousand more important things. Why did those few sentences of my mother's engrave themselves so deeply on my heart? Perhaps because I felt myself capable of thinking and saying them myself, in spite of the violent reprobation they aroused in me. Perhaps because I became conscious of that bent against which I should have to struggle and that I was sadly amazed to discover in my mother. Everything else melted into the harmonious ensemble of her face; and it is perhaps just because I did not recognize her any more by that trait, truly unworthy of her, that my memory took possession of it. What a warning! What strength that educational bent had, then, to triumph in this way from time to time! But my mother remained too surrounded by beings deformed in the same way, to be able to sort out and recognize in herself, among all the acquired characteristics, those spontaneous to her nature; above all, she remained too fearful and unsure of herself to give them the upper hand. She remained worried about others and their opinions; always desirous of the best, but a best answering to accepted rules; always tending toward this best, and without even suspecting (and too modest to recognize it) that the best in her was exactly what she obtained with the least effort.

4

THE DAY OF SEPTEMBER 27

TWO friends came to share my breakfast. The one, a Belgian, a workman from the mines of Borinage, in charge of an inquiry into our departments of the North, was making preparations that very evening and wished to consult me on certain points. The other, my traveling companion in the Congo.

"This Friday, the 27th, is special," I told them, "in that I have to render an exact account of it, and relate all that I have seen and heard in the course of the day." [1]

"If that's the case, I'm going to leave you in the lurch," exclaimed my traveling companion, slipping away immediately.

So did the events. And since, as the consequence of a long period of close application and for more availability, I had very imprudently given myself a

[1] It was on the initiative of Maxim Gorki that on the 27th of September, 1935, in every country in the world, the writers were called upon to describe their day, to note that some event of that day chosen in advance at random, to bring their contribution, under any form whatever, to the collective work to be called "A Day in the Entire World."

holiday on that day, the twenty-four hours flowed by without bringing to my observation anything of note. Thus, in the succession of days, there are certain ones that seem to come only to make up the number and to bring us, by slow degrees, nearer to death. So I find myself face to face with September 27th like a painter to whom one might say suddenly, in the course of a walk: "Sit down there and paint," at just the spot where there would be nothing to paint. He would be reduced to casting a spell over the slightest blade of grass and the stones in the foreground.

Before the arrival of my two friends, I had begun my day with the reading of some poems by Ronsard. The fuller my mind is with the distressing problems of to-day, the more important it is for me to cleanse it each morning and each evening with a bath of contemplation absolutely untimely. I need to preserve in me the feeling of endurance; I mean, the need of feeling there are human things that remain secure from injury and degradation; works upon which the changes of time have no hold. Nothing was less timely than what I was reading. It was simply some beautiful lines that had no other purpose than to fill my heart and mind with a sort of dynamic joy very beneficent. And I thought, on reading them, that one had not, perhaps, remarked sufficiently, at the time of the Writers' Conference, this role of literature: to permit continuity. However far Ronsard's era may seem to me, however indifferent I may be in face of the problems that took up their minds at that time, the emotion that gives life to the *Odes,* because outside the limits of time, remain ever present for me; I wed it and I make it mine at once. I feel comfort and joy in thinking that those who come after will find in this food the same savor.

These reflections have no connection with the date. If I communicate them here it is because they were those of that morning and because I have nothing else to say.

Back in Paris since the previous evening, and as no one yet knew that I was there, I had no fear of being disturbed, and could chat peacefully with my friend, then write a few letters, railing all the while, as every day, against that devouring obligation that correspondence becomes. Then I finished correcting some proofs which I went immediately to take back to the *Nouvelle Revue Française.*

I always carry some printed matter with me, for I like to read as I walk. It is an immaterial screen that one erects between oneself and life; fragile screen, split ceaselessly, for one participates just the same in the bustle of the street; but a special joy comes from the discord between the real and the imaginary. Oh! I am ready to recognize that this habit is contrary to the principles themselves of my ethics; but my ethics also include, most fortunately, inconsistency. So I had taken the last two numbers of the *Littérature Internationale,* that I had just received, anxious to read a novelette by Waldo Frank and the article by Miraki on *The Belle of Basle.* And, by chance, my glance caught my name, in the *Thoughts Outloud* of A. Lejner; which I read immediately with keen pleasure, finding great comfort in that distant and unexpected sympathy.

In the offices of the Revue, I met someone very well informed on the undercurrents of politics, with whom I talked for quite a while, with great interest, certainly, but without much profit, for, in conversations of that kind where I feel the subject escaping my province, the great concern that I have not to appear an idiot makes me immediately become one.

I had lunch alone; then, finding nothing to do, I went to the movies. I am always fond of the movies, but especially after a long stay in the country. I saw an English Colonial picture, dripping with unreality and stupidity, where the whites posed naturally as the champions of courage, of nobility of soul and honor; where the blacks observed as best they could the indications of the stage director to bring out their barbarism. Not all; there was the clan of those who, submissive to English authority and won over to noble sentiments, showed themselves really worthy of becoming British subjects.

Then there was another feature (to tell the truth, it was at the neighborhood theatre, where I went as soon as the colonial picture had ended: I was having a fling!), a French picture, that one; well played, too, and not bad. That film showed, as many others of French production, alas! the painting of moral decay. A pitiful numbskull whom a great paternal love tried to make sympathetic in spite of everything, lent himself, in financial dealings, to the worst forms of complacency, to the filthiest compromises; but this trash took on a sublime air because he committed them for love of the beautiful black eyes of his daughter; with the result that paternal love became as repugnant as love after the manner of des Grieux. I exaggerate, yes, I know; but not much. And, much more than mediocrity, certain forms of complacency in roguery affect me, and the art of finding in love an excuse. If I were not so enamored of the love that exalts, I should not be so resentful of all love that vilifies. And it is this last that, all too often, our literature and our movies like to paint. In three quarters of the novels and pictures that we are offered, it seems that the woman has no other mission than to lead the man into catastrophe.

The picture was, in spite of everything, entertaining and, as I said, well played. It is by the quantity of elements that are mixed in it that a movie attains, with difficulty, the dignity of a work of art; but that is also why we endure, in the movies, a number of productions of a mediocrity whose equivalent we would not accept in literature.

Next I saw (and dare I confess that it was in a third movie-house, where they showed only newsreels?) an official funeral, processions, parades, horse and auto races and, for the third time, for, the public seeming to like it, the two other houses presented also the same ineptitude: a race to see who would get there last. . . . I left filled to the brim. After a long time of work in the country, that debauch found a semblance of excuse in my eyes. In the eyes of others, it's no matter. But still I'm not particularly pleased, since I have to present to the public one day of my life, that that day should do me so little honor.

"It depended only on you to fill it better."

Yes, that's what I kept saying to myself, when evening came and a sort of nausea for all this that I have just said seized me. I hesitated wondering whether I should not recount, instead, the use of my day of the 26th, which had been very happily and usefully stocked; or the next day that, by reaction, I contemplated devoting to work. . . . But I don't like to cheat, and, going home: "It is the emptiness itself of a day of leisure that I must paint," I said to myself, "of a lost day." Yet I haven't so many more to live. So I tried, before having done with the 27th, to get from myself at least a few sublime reflections. . . . Nothing came to me but asinine thoughts. Still it wasn't late. I could give another hour to the revision of the translation of a novel by Jef Last. Then I went over again Ronsard's poems that I had begun to memorize in the morning, testing again and again their soothing action. Then I turned the page of that day, which, in my Journal, would have remained blank, had it not been for the promise I had given to fill it.

5

ACQUASANTA

To my comrade Jef Last.

AND yet the few trips that I took alone were, perhaps, the most profitable for me. I think that a little cowardice enters into that need for a companion, for a pace-maker. Yet as age comes on, it seems to me that I wed a little his youth; it is through him that I feel; thanks to his astonishment I feel surprise once more; I partake of his delight and I know only too well that, when I am alone to enjoy it, the most charming landscapes in the world, the most smiling invitations to joy, are capable of plunging me into a sort of despair. But the memories of all that I enjoyed by proxy, as it were, are more easily detached from me, as though they only half belonged to me; while all that I had to undertake alone, pain or pleasure, remains deeply engraven in my heart.

It was alone that I left at the end of that summer

for the Abruzzi. In what year? I no longer know; but to fix that point, I should only have to look up the date of the publication of the little book by Edmond Gosse, *Critical Kit-Kats,* which had just appeared, that he had sent me, and that was, at that blessed time, my only reading along with the *Paradise Lost* of Milton.

It was, I believe, around the first of September. I was hoping still to have ahead of me a whole season of sea baths in the Adriatic and was very much disappointed, on my arrival at San Benedetto del Tronto, to find all the hotels about to close. In the one in which I put up, I was the only guest, with a young student of uncertain nationality. We didn't speak to each other; and I don't know why, in the immense, deserted dining-room where I took only three meals, our places were set at the two ends of a huge oblong guest table. All during the meals, he and I, face to face, each one buried in his reading, remained without looking at each other. What was he reading that way? I was curious to know and, profiting by a momentary absence on his part, I leaped toward the book he had left on the table; it was *Jerusalem Delivered.* Hastily I regained my place. He came back, and we buried ourselves anew, he in the Tasso, I in the Milton.

Yes, the season had ended. The bath-houses no longer cluttered up the huge beach where I was wandering about, my heart full of expectation and anxiety, repeating to myself the lines of Laforgue:

Here comes autumn . . .
The casinos that are deserted
Put away their pianos . . .

Without any more bathers or tourists, the little city took back its normal aspect; the fishing smacks were leaving the port, two by two, with curious insignia, multi-colored figures recalling those of heraldry; one couple bore a besant of gold on a field of gules, another couple a sable cross on a field of sinople, others great parti-colored emblems; all that spread out in splendor over the cerulean carpet of the sea, evoking the times of the Crusades and a whole glorious past. I saw them fade in the distance, gain the open sea; I should have liked to see their return, I could not even imagine them bringing back any other fish than red mullets or dolphins, or some fabulous marine monsters. But I left the next day for Acquasanta, where I knew I was to find, if not sea baths, a pool of sulphur water for a cure that I had prescribed for myself, in which to store up a health reserve to get through the winter. The train went only as far as Ascoli; I then had to take the stage to Acquila. Acquasanta is along the first quarter of the routine that crosses the Abruzzi. I don't recall this route clearly enough to be able to describe any of it.

At Acquasanta I learned the hotel had been closed for several days as the season was over. Not knowing where else to stay, I obtained permission from the keeper of the hotel to be lodged there; he consented to get ready for me one of the pleasantest rooms in it. He himself did not live in the hotel; so he entrusted me with the key, advising me to put on the night lock every evening. A spare key permitted his wife to bring me bread and coffee every morning. As for the midday and evening meals, he confessed it would be rather difficult to vary them; I would have to content myself with very little. But what did that matter! I have retained a delightful memory of the daily salads of sweet pimentos; not those orange pimentos, red or yellow, that I admired on the market squares, but little pimentos of a joyous, elementary green, fruits that I had never tasted, that, the first day, seemed horrible to me, but to which I became so well accustomed that to-day I deplore not being able to digest them.

The country was marvelous. When I think of Italy, it seems to me immediately that there is no country in the world I prefer; but never until then had she appeared to me of such captivating grace. Many charming paths, disappearing into the folds of the mountains, led to villages not too distant that each offered some surprising specialty. It was harvest time; an unusual gaiety animated all the peasants; when I passed by them, they held out to me the bunch of grapes they had just picked from the arbor, or that they were gathering, either in the little handcart they were pulling, or in the basket they carried on their backs to take the harvest to the wine-press; round about the villages, the heady perfume of must was already filling the air. Amidst laughing and singing, young men, barefooted and barearmed, crushed the grapes in the vats, as one can see it done at Campo Santo di Pisa, in the fresco of Benozzo Gozzoli. I tarried near them until evening. The narrow valley was then filling up with shadows and haze. Above, and by contrast no doubt, the air was becoming, it seemed, more sonorous, more limpid, more crystalline, and from one village to the next, long, joyous calls reechoed. Ah! How far I felt myself from Paris, and how little I wished to go back!

But what kept me at Acquasanta, more than the beauty of the country and the perfume of the harvest, was the child with whom I had fallen in love. I met him only at the baths; and before speaking of him, I must describe the pool. In this post season it was frequented only by the natives of the country who had free access to it after the first of September; poor people who had the right to be sick too. But some, and among them Bernardino, took baths for the pleasure of it. As for me, I had decided that, having missed a season of sea baths, a cure in the sulphur pools would cure me of any future ills. Foreigners had to have a medical authorization, but the obliging doctor discovered, at my request, an indisposition that only the waters of Acquasanta could combat.

The pool? It was a subterranean lake—it was a little lake that my memory magnifies—not very deep, of which the sun reached only the right bank and which, under a shady vault, spread out, stretched out wide at first, then continued to narrow as it got farther from the light up to the steep wall in the background, that on entering one could scarcely see. There, in the very back, flowed out, in an abundant cascade, the thermal waters; they did not burst directly from the rock but were carried from a distant point by a channel half way up the wall which one could scale, it was said, but where I never dared risk myself, for in the depths of the lake the heat was already suffocating. Engirdling the lake, a continuous row of benches had been cut into the stone, so one could sit down there while keeping his head out of the water. This water was of an indescribable color, bluish-green and milky at the same time (I imagined just like it the color of sirens' milk), completely opaque; the bodies disappeared entirely, which permitted bathing without a costume.

No matter how soon I arrived at the pool in the morning, Bernardino had always gotten there first. From the first day I had noticed him, the only child among the bathers. He might have been fourteen years of age, perhaps fifteen. His dark hair, of medium length, half covered his slightly pug-nosed face; through the disorderly matted locks that the water carried forward, his eyes shone; the least smile immediately revealed his teeth. One would have said a triton had escaped the voluptuous cortege of Amphitrite, and the water seemed his element. His extraordinarily rapid swimming was like a dance, divided between the crawl and the mazurka, but it recalled still more the capering behaviour of the seals and dolphins that, even in the calmest water, seem now buoyed up by an imaginary wave, now to fall pirouetting into the billows; and the bound that brought him up uncovered his delicate shoulder for an instant. The first day I spoke to him, I was astonished at all I could find to say to him with the few words of Italian I knew. But I am only a wretched swimmer and, when we swam together, got out of breath quickly and let myself be outdistanced at once. If, when he let me catch up with him, I tried to seize him, he swam away with a ringing laugh, diving suddenly, and I didn't see him reappear until he was far away. However, he answered my questions as good-naturedly as possible and seemed to take pleasure in chatting. I learned that he was the oldest of a rather large family; his father was cobbler and cultivator at the same time. But Bernardino refused to let me know where he lived, as well as to permit me to meet him any place except at the pool, protesting in addition that his parents would not tolerate his taking up with a stranger; and on saying this, he affected a filial submission and veneration so excessive that he could not keep himself from smiling at it immediately, as if to let me understand that malice and challenge entered into his reticence. Then he questioned me: What had I come to do there, in this post season when no one met anyone any more? And I got all mixed up in a sentence trying to tell him that his society was enough for me and that it pleased me much more than that of the people of high society. How long would I stay? Then I felt my glance become tender and told him that, near him, I could not dream of leaving.

I would have liked to see him leave the pool; but in vain I prolonged my baths, in vain I watched for him to come out. The way in which he escaped me remained incomprehensible, with the result that there entered into that lover's chase a little challenge. In the afternoon, all the charm of the walks was needed to distract my thought from him a little. But when, in the evening, I tried to return to Milton, I thought I would have done just as well to bring Virgil with me.

However Bernardino did not fail to be impressed by my constancy, and all the more as he saw very well that I spoke to no one except him. Twelve days had already fled and I was thinking with gloom and distress of all that was soon going to recall me to France. . . .

On that day, the thirteenth of my stay (I have always been favored by the thirteenth), as I had, in swimming, reached the deepest shade of the grotto, Bernardino, without my having called him, came to join me. I sat down on the stone bench near the cascade. And suddenly Bernardino was in my lap, hugging me with his charming arms, putting his chin on my shoulder, hiding his eyes against my neck and pressing his forehead to my cheek. How light that little body was!

And at first I wasn't worried, thinking that he owed his lack of weight to the old law of Archimedes. My hands were still lagging behind feeling his back; ah! how my heart turned over suddenly when my caress as it descended, discovered that his left leg stopped at the beginning of his thigh; the slim member over which my hand was preparing to slip lovingly was only a stump.

Poor Bernardino! At once I understood your retreats, your flights, your strange swimming, your well-being in the opaque waters, protectors of your secret; and now your confusion, and, pressed against my shoulder your face that you did not want to raise any more. . . .

To how many kisses did I have to have recourse, to how many caresses, to have confidence finally come liven up his eyes, and a smile once more to his trembling lips! How many protestations and oaths before convincing him that his painful deformity did not repel my love too much! A great tenderness now filled my heart, and I persuaded myself that I loved him all the more; but that tenderness immediately made me understand how painfully he would be wounded by an alteration, a change to pity, in my desires. Pity, to be sure! Commiseration, that's what he met everywhere along his road and that sort of charitable love that hovers over misfortune. (Later he informed me that his parents loved him dearly, that they were sympathetic with him in the village, that he had received care and help from public relief.) Everything with which they flooded him always reminded him of his misfortune. But that anyone could still fall in love with his beauty, his charm, that he could awaken desire, in spite of everything, that is what opened a new heaven to him by reconciling him to himself. No, Bernardino, it is not pity I offer you, but ardor.

Now that I knew everything, that he no longer

had to fear my look, he made no more fuss about leaving the water in front of me. Outside of the water his body resumed once more its unequal weight. Dragging himself woefully, he went to get his clothing and an indispensable crutch. I took great care to keep on smiling at him, although my heart was indignant. He smiled too, but sadly, and, as soon as he was dressed, I distinguished on his countenance an expression of sadness and suffering that contorted his features a little and that I had never before noticed, either because the darkness of the pool hid it from me or, because in swimming he lost it with the feeling of his pain. He let me go home with him; introduced me to his family. By the manner in which I was received, I understood he had spoken of me. As for the claimed severity of his father, his refusal to let him go with me, he did not speak of it any more except to laugh about it. He related to me without too much bitterness the ordinary accident that had broken his leg, then the blundering care of an incompetent surgeon, the leg badly set, kept too long in the plaster cast, the beginning of gangrene, the amputation judged necessary. . . . That had been four years before.

It was only in his family that I could appreciate Bernardino's charm, his good nature with his brothers, his obligingness with everyone. In the pool one would have thought him another being, laughing, joking, mischievous and liberated. I loved those two Bernardinos with very different loves; my feeling for the terrestrial Bernardino became purified, but I think he preferred what I felt for the Bernardino of the pool; at least, in the water he showed himself more friendly, more winning, more wanton and tenderly voluptuous.

What became of him? I don't know. Five days after I had to leave Acquasanta to which I never returned.

6

DINDIKI

PERODICTIQUE POTTO: That is how the scholars have baptised him. He has no other name in our language. But I called him Dindiki[1], the name the natives over there gave him.

This little animal, although belonging to the family of primates, bears almost no resemblance to the monkey. He would remind you much more of a hedge-hog with soft hair, or a very little bear, a pocket-bear.

He is a climber. Native of the equatorial forest, he lives in the inaccessible tops of tall trees. He is, besides, a nocturnal animal. For those two reasons he remains difficult to catch; but, on the other hand, he is very slow and does not seem to be afraid of man. If he is not seen more often it is, I believe, because he is rather rare. As soon as I had understood what a charming animal Dindiki was, I sent some men out to find a companion for him. I already imagined

[1] The *n* is pronounced.

the couple in France; he was founding a family and I was offering a little pérodictique to Larbaud. In spite of the promised rewards to the native huntsmen, they came back after failing completely.

Dindiki had been given me by the chief of Zaoro-Yanga, a little village north of Nola. He was still very young. In the hen-coop of woven reeds, in which he was then enclosed, he looked like a fat rat; and I hesitated to accept him not having any inkling of his good disposition. But, from the first day, I saw he was not savage; let out of his coop, he did not try to run away. For three weeks I thought it prudent, nevertheless, to keep him on a leash, at the end of a string attaching one of his paws to my chair, to my hammock or my bed. But he was soon able to persuade me that this tying-up was unnecessary and that the adoption was reciprocal. From then on he lived close to me, against me, in my lap, on my shoulder. I was probably his tree; a tree that walks and takes you where you don't want to go. . . . Dindiki, my constant little companion throughout that long voyage, to-day I still miss and regret you. O living memory of the great equatorial forest and its shadowy charm! When, after seven months of friendship, a little before arriving at Douala where we were to embark, you left me for some other world, it was to all that distant country that, at the same time, I said goodbye.

On my return to Paris, I found some pérodictiques in the galleries of the Museum, but stuffed, and the naturalists told me that they had never seen any living ones. Before speaking of his customs, I am going to try to describe him.

The pérodictique's coat is of an ashen gray-brown. The hair, lighter and softer on the stomach, becomes, as it nears the middle of the back, almost rough; particularly along the neck and the shoulders, it completely covers up the very prominent apophyses of his cervical vertebrae. It is the peculiarity of his anatomy that naturalists point out as the most noticeable; at the height of the shoulder blades, seven protuberant vertebrae form a crest or saw teeth. Perhaps the apophyses make a hole in the skin with age, as some say; but the skin still completely covered up Dindiki's. I read, too, that these peculiar protuberances, hidden, as I have said, by the hair, but very noticeable to the finger, served doubtless as a means of support to the pérodictique, and that he dug them into a flaw of the bark when he was preparing to go to sleep. That does not appear very probable to me. I think more likely that he uses them as a sort of snout when, sticking his head between his front paws as the hedgehogs do, and arching his back, he advances, as I have seen him do, to frighten a not very redoubtable enemy (it was a little dog) or to charge upon an obstacle. It is also with his head folded between his paws and all rolled up in a ball that he sleeps; the very long hair at his neck warns him of the least unusual contact.

His nose is not more elongated than the bear's. Of his eyes can be seen only a reddish-brown iris; almost no pupil; the diaphragm is closed during the day. The arch of his eyebrow shows a slight protuberance, more perceptible to the finger than to the eye; it surrounds the eye with a wide parenthesis, as fine as the crescent of the moon on the first day of rhamadan. The rounded spirals of his tiny little ears are drowned in hair; he has the incisors of the rodent and the canines of his upper jaw developed and apparent.

His paws . . . but the word "paw" is inappropriate; he has arms and legs and hands. Four hands of which it is not enough to say the thumb is opposable; this very long thumb does not form an angle with the other fingers but just prolongs the index of the hands behind, and the third finger of the hands in front; for, on the front paws, the index finger is lacking, exists no longer, except as a little stump of an index scarcely raising the skin.

His nails are short, like those of the monkey, except that on the index finger of the hands behind, which, as though to compensate for the absence of the index finger on the hands on front, is extremely long, forming a claw which he uses for scratching.

Thanks to the disposition of his thumbs and his musculature, his hug is formidable. The natives affirm that he strangles animals much larger than himself, monkeys in particular, which he surprises in their sleep. When he clutches a branch, he can not be made to let go; he would sooner be quartered; he gets mad if you insist, tries to bite and utters furious cries. He has that in common with the little loris, sloth of the Sunda Islands that, I think, resembles him closely; but Oken [1] tells us that the latter gives off a repulsive odor, which is not the case with Dindiki.

Like the loris, the pérodictique only gets around slowly; "slow and deliberate in his movements," says Christy who speaks of him very pertinently but incidentally, in his remarkable work on the animals of the equatorial forest. He never opens his front hand until the corresponding back hand is first assured of its prey. The bound is contrary to his ethics. *"Natura non fecit saltus"* is his rule of conduct, and *"Festinare non decet."* You could say he proceeds by syllogisms. If you want to make him hurry, he turns toward you, protests with little cries, irritated as though you were cutting the thread of his reason.

He is agile only when he climbs. On the ground his movements are awkward, comical; he advances

[1] Oken, *Allgemeine Naturgeschichte.*

with the little trot of the plantigrade, with the affectation of Charlie Chaplin. Then only he begins to hurry; he runs toward the trunk of a tree, the first in sight, or toward a leg; his hands grip it, his limbs give enormous hugs with both arms and legs; in no time at all he raises himself; there he is again on my shoulder; he puts his arms around my neck, his nose against my cheek. (The power to kiss is the permission for tenderness). You wait for him to purr; but each being has his particular eloquence; by his caress Dindiki makes me know he is happy.

My hair has much more attraction for him than my face; doubtless he finds in it a more vegetable appearance; doubtless he considers my hairy skin like a sort of hairy bark; he does not lick as much as he scratches, very gently with his long front teeth; you would say he wanted to skin me. But the light bothers him; he slips into my half open shirt, and there, soon all relaxed, everything abandoned, absolutely tranquil, protected from the wind, the sun, from being seen, he falls asleep. I can walk, ride horse-back, hunt, he'll not budge any more until evening. The food I offer him draws him out of his beatific drowsiness a little, but he plunges back into it again immediately.

It is not even at sunset, but two hours after, that he awakes. He stretches himself. He nibbles me a little, as though to assure me again of his presence. He comes out of his hiding place, sniffs the air less burning, weighted with perfume and moisture. How good it is! It is the time when the pupils of his eyes that do not close at night, become enlarged, when the sky gives back to the earth a little of the humidity it has taken from it, when the forest begins to live. For Dindiki, it is the time to come down from his roost. I imagine him descending from the top of his tree, reaching the spring where he quenches his thirst. I imagine a family of dindikis, father, mother and little ones, all in single file as is the custom of the country, that custom followed by the giraffes, antelopes and the natives, and that we adopt over there, for there is nothing to do but submit to the customs whose reason is hidden from us. I see them with that little brisk, joking air they know how to assume and that amused me so much; I see them passing from one tree to another, from branch to branch, or making the creepers bend under their light weight. The father guides them toward the cavity the bees have filled with honey. At this time the bees are asleep; and if they happen to stir, the dindikis roll themselves into a ball; the sting is not as long as their hair. They play jokes; they gloat. . . .

Alas! it is the time when I must shut up Dindiki; for it is the time when he emancipates himself; he escapes me; he would like to run after adventure;

and it would be to find what? We left the forest a long time ago; the country we are crossing is only a gloomy savannah, where famine cries aloud, where one looks in vain for shelter. Would he really like to leave me? Perhaps not; but only run a little. When I let him wander about in my whaler, if we are navigating on the Logone or the Chari, he never fails to return to me; makes unbelievable efforts to join me. When, worn out, I isolate him in the boys' whaler, he passes from one to the other, over the cable that ties them together. He makes the ascension of my armchair, from behind, slyly and, as a joke, from the top of the back, he pulls my hair or my ear; that means: "Play with me." Or hanging by one foot on the *shimbeck,* his body stretched out unbelievably, with his forepaw he reaches my skull and scratches it a minute, then runs away. But the most fun (for him at any rate, for I would like to sleep) is, as soon as he sees me lying down, to do acrobatic stunts on the top of my mosquito net, turn somersaults, curl up, and what not! How gay he is! Then he goes round and round the closed net, with which he gets very impatient; he tries to slip under it; he succeeds. All that is charming; but when, after a long day of walking, I would like to get a little momentum from sleep for to-morrow's walk, I shut Dindiki in a basket or in one of the sleeping bags; from which, in the morning, he comes out briskly, and, once delivered, pitter-patters toward me without resentment.

In the early days, I intended, by keeping him awake during the day, to triumph over his habits, to induce him to sleep at night. He didn't understand. That almost caused a break between us. Besides, he just didn't sleep all day long, only he was quiet. When I walked or went horseback, he seemed to take great pleasure in seeing the road unroll, in seeing himself taken from place to place without effort. He was afraid of nothing. When I took him hunting, the noise of gunshots, so close to him, didn't even make him tremble.

He was one of the easiest to feed, ate great quantities of bread, and as willingly rice or cassava. Condensed milk, cooked creams, preserves, were his favorite food; but all constipating foods, with the result that I did not dare give in too much to his tastes. On a certain evening when we were at table with him, our lamps attracted a swarm of winged termites that all at once drove him crazy. He threw himself on them with a sort of rage; and to see him eat them that way (the natives eat them too) gave me the idea of offering him other insects. He crunched them all, almost indifferently at first; but the black beetles disgusted him; shaking his head violently, he spit out all he could with a great abundance of saliva; and, after that, we stuck to tiger beetles.

However, in spite of all my care, I never succeeded in giving him food that was not over-heating; for he refused almost all fruits; and even those he accepted, banana or papaya, he touched only with the ends of his teeth; so that, from time to time, I had to resort to injections.

Constipation was not the only thing from which he was to suffer. The heat tried him very much. It must be said that, in the damp equatorial forest where he lived, the temperature rarely rises above 35 degrees[1]. Between Pouss and Maroua, in the north of the Cameroons, we were crossing a region without shade. Everything was dry, burnt up, consumed. Each day, we started on our way long before dawn to avoid the most torrid hours. At Gingleï, which we reached the 21st of March, after six hours of walking, the thermometer registered 45 degrees[1] at the coolest spot in the passenger compartment, a round hut, with a roof of thatch, or palms, or reeds, supported by a bundle of branches. Both Marc and I, prostrate in our steamer-chairs, panted for breath. Contrary to his habit, Dindiki tried to escape me. Tired of holding on to him, of running after him, of getting him back, I ended by letting him alone.

[1] Centigrade. Translator's note.

He reached the nearest beam, then the branches of the roof, then, going higher and higher, almost disappeared in the dusty tangle of twigs. Evidently the little animal hoped, by going up, to find a little coolness, as, in his native forest, at the breezy tops of high trees. But his instinct deceived him here; under the oven-heated roof, in the depths of that funnel without exit, it was hell. And stupidly (I was exhausted) I told myself: "If he's too hot, he'll come down." Dindiki didn't come down. On the contrary, at two different times, I saw him force himself further into that gehenna. Still I add, to my credit, and so as not to be judged too much of an idiot, that Dindiki, ordinarily, did not seem to suffer much from a lack of air. It often happened that he buried himself under cushions and blankets, that he slipped way down into my bed, "to the extreme limit of suffocation," Madrus would have said; as, if to sleep well, the *non spirare* should be added to the *non vedere* and the *non sentire;* in this way life is suspended by certain fakirs and hibernating animals. And this habit of the pérodictique permits me to believe that he must make his nest in the cavities of old trees, or perhaps he enters to hide during the day, in the manner of our dormice and lerots. . . . I return to Gingleï. We had still a rather long trek to complete before evening. When the moment came to start again, I asked Outhman, one of our two boys, to go find Dindiki for me. He brought down from the top of the roof a little soft, inert mass with sightless eyes and a heart that was scarcely beating any more.

I would not admit that Dindiki was dead. I laid him on my lap, breathed on him, rubbed him, and while Outhman fanned him, gave him, with Marc's aid, the artificial respiration with which one resuscitates the drowned. Marc had the idea of an injection of caffeine. Adoum, our other boy, ran after the porters, going along up ahead with the canteens, and brought back our pharmacy chest. At the end of an hour of treatment, his heart began to beat again. He vomited, which seemed a good sign to us and appeared to mark the refunctioning of his organs. Death had at last released its grip.

Dindiki took a long time to recover. The heat continued to be overpowering. Around his coop I put a damp cloth over which a big sponge slowly dripped water. For six days he refused any other food or drink except the saliva he came to gather from my lip, like Lesbia's sparrow. He showed himself extraordinarily eager for it, by appetite, greediness . . . or tenderness; for since his asphyxia, he had become still more affectionate, as if he understood I had snatched him from death. Alas! I did not succeed in fighting effectively against the constipation that finally took him away from me two months later. Those periods of stoppage were followed by collapses that forced me to exile him for a time in a basket. He came out of it terribly embarrassed, for there was no one cleaner or more careful of his person than that little being. Certainly something was lacking in his diet, grass, bark, that I could not get for him. I even persuaded myself that in the latter days, it was to hunt for it, that he was so anxious to run about. He seemed to say to me: "Why no! I don't want to escape. Only let me find that. I will come back." That, what was it? I thought I had found it when I saw him throw himself greedily on a tree gum Outhman had brought me. But only the next day, he didn't want any more. He showed himself more and more difficult, as if he had understood that the food I was offering him, and with which he was satisfied at first, was not exactly what suited him. I saw him with anxiety and despair refuse, turn about, bread, rice and semolina. When I was going across the brush, he hung himself from one of my fingers, by a paw, and stayed head down, brushing against the grass; and I walked very slowly, lingering in the hope of seeing him snatch at a blade suddenly. Nevertheless, up to the next to the last day, he stayed in a charming mood, as affectionate as ever. He begged for my caress, raising his little arms up very high to invite me to scratch his armpit; and he even crossed his two hands above his head with the gesture of a ballerina. . . . Then, suddenly he began to hate me; two different times, he bit me cruelly; without reasoning exactly, he persuaded himself, I am sure, that I was what prevented him from taking care of himself in his own way, what had taken him away, what had kept him far from his blessed forest. He understood that I could not cure him.

The last day, Dindiki couldn't walk any more except painfully, leaning over on one side; I felt him suffer. I did not take my eyes from him. It was between my hands that he died, without a moan, like a little child who falls asleep.

7

JOSEPH CONRAD

"I WONDER if it is the end," I read in a letter dated the 30th of May, the last I received from him; as cordial as usual, and pierced like the others by a sort of harsh playfulness, by a somewhat grumpy charm, which gave a rather briny savor to the outbursts of his sympathy; but already imprinted with the mysterious gravity and presentiment of death.

That letter cut me to the heart like a farewell. I felt myself in arrears with him. I had remained too long a time without seeing him again or writing him. Had I ever been able to tell him, what I wrote him immediately, of all the affection, the admiration and veneration that, in spite of so much absence and silence, I had never ceased to devote to him? Of my elders, I loved and knew only him.

"It is four years since I have done anything worth while. On the other hand, I have asthma. It's pretty annoying. What consoles me is the success (moderate, I agree) of the French translations."

Conrad loved France much too deeply not to attach the greatest value to the opinion of the French about his work. This was not yet known except to a small number of admirers. The announcement of his death was needed before the press would finally consent to be moved. They seemed suddenly to understand whom we were losing.

It was Claudel who made Conrad known to me. I remain indebted to him for it. After a lunch we had had together, as some one of the other guests was speaking with enthusiasm of Kipling, Claudel smiled a little disdainfully and threw in the name of Conrad. Not one of us knew it yet.

"What should I read of his?" asked someone.

"Everything," answered Claudel. And he quoted *The Nigger of the Narcissus, Youth, Typhoon, Lord Jim*. . . . None of these books had yet been translated. I immediately made a note of their titles, and was won over from the very first contact with them.

A short time after, while traveling in England, I had the opportunity of coming directly in contact with their author. Valéry Larbaud was accompanying me (if my memory does not betray me). Miss Tobin, a charming young Englishwoman whom Larbaud knew, was to introduce us to him. Conrad was then living in Kent, at Capel House, a little country house in the neighborhood of Ashford; that is where he received us. I lingered several days with him; I returned to Capel House the following year, and there was soon established between us the warmest and most lively friendship.

Conrad did not like to speak of his past life; a sort of modesty or ill-will toward himself restrained him, prevented his making confidences. His seafaring memories appeared nothing more to him than matter to make up; and, a certain artistic exigency mingling with it, forcing him to transpose it, to depersonalize and push away from him by means of fiction everything that concerned him personally, in his books as well as in his conversation, he was remarkably unskillful in direct narration; it was only in fiction that he felt at ease.

The sea was for him like a deserted former mistress, and, in the waiting-room of Capel House, only an engraving of it, the picture of a superb sailboat, evoked nostalgic memories.

"Don't look at that," he said to me, leading me into the reception-room while I was contemplating the symbol of his first love. "Let's talk about literature."

Conrad had married, "settled down"; he lived with his wife and children, by and for his books. How well he knew our authors! He admired Flaubert and Maupassant, whose praises he gladly sang.

He had a particular taste for our critics, especially Jules Lemâitre. He esteemed Barrès only moderately; you can imagine what he would think of the theories of expatriation, perfect expatriot that he was. As he never expressed an opinion on anything except with unfailing competence, his judgments were sure; but as they agreed with mine, the conversation continued for a long time without a clash. On one point only, we were unable to come to an understanding; the very name of Dostoyefsky made him pale. I think some journalists, by inept comparisons, had heated the exasperation of the Pole against the great Russian; with whom, notwithstanding, he did not fail to present certain resemblances, but whom he detested cordially and of whom one could not speak in front of him without renewing his vehement indignation. I should have liked to understand what he reproached in his books, but I never obtained anything from him except vague imprecations.

The first evening I passed at Capel House, the discussion just missed becoming tempestuous. But this time I joined the chorus with him. Miss Tobin would not allow herself to praise Georges Ohnet to the skies? We protested. She remained obstinate, defending her man with arguments that appeared to us absurd, monstrous, speaking of "the temperate outburst," the "dull richness," of his paintings. Conrad became more and more excited up to the moment when Miss Tobin called Walter Pater to her aid and we suddenly understood that it was a question, not of the author of the too celebrated *Mâitre de Forges,* (*Master of the Forge*), but indeed of Giorgione, whose name she pronounced in Italian, in such a way as to permit the misunderstanding. It had lasted almost an hour. Conrad was as amused by it as a child.

Nothing was more cordial, more forthright, more manly than his laugh, his expression and his voice. But, like the sea during a lull, you felt him capable of violent passions, of storms. However great his curiosity might be for the secret retreats of the human soul, he hated everything sly, underhanded or vile of which man was capable. And I think what I liked most in him, was a sort of native nobility, harsh, disdainful, and somewhat despairing, which he lends to Lord Jim and which makes the book one of the most beautiful I know, one of the saddest also, and, at the same time, one of the most uplifting.

Others than I will speak of the teaching that can be derived from his work, since for that matter it is the style to-day to look for lessons everywhere. I think Conrad's is most profitable in an era when, on the one hand, the study of man tends to distract novelists from life, and on the other, the love of life tends to discredit literature. No one had lived more brutally than Conrad; no one, afterwards, had submitted life to so patient, conscientious and learned a transmutation of art.

8

FRANCIS JAMMES

I MYSELF am too near the tomb "by affliction and years" to be able to grieve much over his death. This success of the Good God that Jammes was, fully completed his task and, for many years past, his slipping toward Paradise was only too perceptible in his work and in his life. Should I say even that this affliction brings me one satisfaction: that of being able to let him figure in the anthology of French poets which I am preparing (and where no living men are to figure) with an abundant choice from his work.

Francis Jammes had full consciousness of his importance; in the contemporary literary movement, it is considerable and can justify his pride. I think he needed this pride to permit him to assert himself, and from his very first poems, with such an unyielding originality. Jammes made a clean break with the schools and poetic tradition. His work is not a continuation of anything; it starts anew and from the ground up; it is a spring where the thirsty, or "the pure in heart" come to drink. Jammes is delightfully genuine. And what makes it more surprising is that, for songs so new, he used the old alexandrine; but he used it with such determined lack of skill, that the old instrument, put out of tune by him, made the sounds unrecognizable.

Le pauvre pion doux, si sale, m'a dit: j'ai
Bien mal aux yeux et le bras droit paralysé . . .
Il économise pour se faire soigner. . . .[1]

Anyone can try new harmonies; the special property of Jammes was to bring his novelty to perfection immediately. For that matter, this novelty was not artificially obtained; it was so as not to put his voice out of tune that he put the instrument out of tune; that was all that counted with him: that his voice should be true. That of Francis Jammes did not recall any other; as genuine as the human voice can be. Now we are accustomed to it, it does not surprise us any more; when the first poems of the man who called himself a faun appeared, that voice at first seemed discord to the ears of the cultivated city folk; but soon, the exact pitch of that voice tri-

---

[1] *The poor, gentle dominie, so dirty, said to me: "My eyes hurt so much, and my right arm is paralysed." He economises to have himself treated. . . .* Translator's note.

umphed and, alongside of it, it was the voice of his contemporaries that appeared artificial, borrowed.

Jammes did not have to search. The first letters I received from him show him, from 1893, still young, already fully conscious of his savor, his virility, his gifts, with all his charming faults, his resolute obtuseness, his pride and fantasy, his irreplaceable qualities. I thought that, more than my commentaries, some of his letters from years long gone by, would deservedly interest the readers of the *N. R. F.* in spite of the oddities of the dithyrambs. I am adding to them some personal recollections, written a few years ago. I give them without adding anything. I should like to be able to make felt, through certain reserves, the affection that bound us and which holds such a great place in my life.

REDISCOVERED PAGES

I had already been in correspondence with him for a long time, when he came to join us at Biskra where we, my wife and I, were completing our wedding trip. He let himself be brought there by a mutual friend, Eugène Rouart, eager to introduce us to each other and to make him see the country; for he had never yet left Orthez. In our letters, we used the *tu* form; but when I saw getting out of the train that sprightly little being, bearded, with a ringing voice and a gimlet eye, I found him so little like what I had imagined him to be, that the *tu* at first gave place to *vous;* which seemed to have such an effect on him that the *tu* was taken up again.

He had taken me by the arm, very affectionately, as soon as we had found ourselves alone, on the terrace of the hotel, but I was not a little surprised by the protecting and even contemptuous tone that he assumed on speaking to me of Eugène Rouart, for whom I had much more affection than he seemed to think, and with whom I was more intimate than I could ever be with Jammes. Convinced that, no more than he, could I doubt for an instant the immense superiority of both of us over our mutual friend, he gave me to understand at once he feared that superiority would soon get our poor friend into a most painful situation.

"We should," he said to me, "watch our remarks carefully, and say nothing too subtle in front of him, so as not to mortify him."

The attention was, most assuredly, delicate, but showed such a lack of understanding of others, that I was embarrassed, to such a degree I did not know what to say to him. As apparent as that great fault was, yet one did not suffer too much because of it, for Jammes was a charming fellow and, at that time, did not pontificate at all. His good spirits were extraordinary. It was one continuous outburst of anecdotes about the bourgeoisie of Pau and Orthez. He narrated delightfully and with such art that one never tired of listening to him. He had parading before you a surprising quantity of puppets with preposterous gestures and droll comments, that appeared to him (and that he showed) all the more extravagant since he saw, in those he painted, only the outside.

When, the next summer, he came to pass some time with us at La Roque, my old Aunt Demarest, who did not unbend easily, was sometimes ill with laughter. But first I come back to Biskra; in addition to his talent as a story-teller, Jammes had the gift of analogies, a gift that he often confused with poetic genius. His nerves always tingling seemed like the cords of a lute that would reverberate at the approach of every harmony; he amused himself with it; he asked, pointing to an object, when we were out for a walk:

"What does that recall to you? What does that make you think of?"—and amused us by the most unexpected analogies, most surprisingly exact, but of which none of the rest of us would have thought.

We lingered only a few more days at Biskra, then left for Touggourt, where we were to separate, for, aided by fatigue, the misunderstanding between

Jammes and Rouart soon became intolerable. Jammes left us there. He left all alone, and his departure was pathetic. He was to return at once to Orthez and was persuaded he was decidedly not made to leave home. However, he readily consented to come to La Roque, and I have very pleasant memories of his stay with us.

Ghéon was our guest when Jammes came to join us. To tease him a little about his knowledge of natural history, that he liked to advance, and which did not appear to me very exact, we had agreed, Ghéon and I, to call the wasps "scorpion-fish." There was a great abundance of them at that season: they entered by the open window of the dining-room, where, as soon as Jammes was seated, Ghéon exclaimed:

"Another scorpion-fish!"

Jammes, who saw nothing more than a wasp, surprised and disturbed, confessed his ignorance. "Scorpion-fish and wasp! Can they be confused? There is no relationship between them!" But soon Jammes joined our game, to find that the name *scorpion-fish* indeed fitted them very much better; then, starting off, he proposed rebaptising many things, and finding for each object a name unexpectedly adequate. Thus we framed an extraordinary lexicon that entertained us all through his stay; eye-glasses became *cavalry;* a watch-key, a *time-jack;* some rather mediocre bordeau that my wife was serving at table was called *outsider;* but a rather remarkable burgundy was baptised by Jammes "nipon." For this little game, the names found by him always seemed to us the best.

Jammes showed himself extremely attentive to my Aunt Demarest; rather flattered, moreover, I think, by the success he had with her; entertaining himself by making her laugh and sometimes shocking her a little.

"Madame Demarest, what does this remind you of?" he asked her at table, pointing out with his finger a peach, in a fruit dish, that a slug had spoiled considerably; it was a sort of peculiar cavity, yellowish and very ugly looking. My aunt fixed her "cavalry" on her nose, leaned over, examined a little, then declared simply that it didn't remind her of anything. So Jammes, in his ringing voice, declared:

"The foramen of the priest's ear."

"Ah, Monsieur Jammes . . ."

And the servant who was serving us, bent double, stifled her laughter in a napkin.

After supper we organized a little game of *squails* around the big table in the reception room. They were little quoits of black and white box-wood that had to be thrown with a flip as near as possible to a metal jack, standing in the middle of the table, dislocating the opponents as much as possible, and playing the game with partners. Jammes called my aunt "the Talleyrand of the blacks," which flattered her a great deal, for she played skillfully.

My aunt did not get up early, but when we took a walk in front of the house after breakfast, she could sometimes be seen at her bedroom window. She was a little near-sighted, and didn't even see the deep bow Ghéon made to her. So Jammes said to him:

"Useless, dear friend. . . . Madame Demarest doesn't recognize anybody before ten o'clock in the morning."

That was the time she came down. But before that we had already left for our walk.

One day when Ghéon, Jammes and I had driven to Trouville, and were walking rapidly on the beach, Jammes, particularly excited, became suddenly worried; his face darkened; his eyes filled with tears. His silence bothered us, for until then he had not stopped talking. . . .

"No, there is nothing the matter with me. . . . But suddenly, I surprised a heliotrope scent. . . . And that scent awakens memories in me. . . ."

Then silence again; a silence we respected, and the walk ended without any one of us three saying a word. On our return, Jammes shut himself up in his room. And it was that night he composed one of his most beautiful *Elegies* (*"In the abandoned domain where the great wind . . ."*).

That elegy referred to another walk we had taken

the evening before, in an "abandoned domain," which served later as the scene for my *Isabelle*. Almost everything I relate in that book is authentic, and, when I was younger, I might have known the remarkable inhabitants of that chateau which I called "la Quartfourche," and that, in reality, is called Formentin.

The next morning, when Jammes read me the lines he had composed during the night, as great as might be my admiration, I could not refrain from pointing out to him some imperfections that seemed to me to detract a little from his poem. He retired to fix it up; came back at the end of an hour:

"Dear friend," he said to me, "I wanted to correct it but . . . I don't know whether I have the right."

I remained for a few moments without understanding. However, the sense of the words was clear: this poem having been written under the dictation of inspiration, every touching-up should be considered impious. Indeed, one can not imagine a mind more incapable of criticism, of himself as well as of others. And even the word "incapable" seems to me inexact. The spirit of criticism, according to Jammes, was always an attack on liberty, and immediately blanched love, religion and poetry.

I again encountered this self-sufficiency, later, under particularly painful circumstances. Charles-Louis Philippe had just died. The *N. R. F.* immediately prepared a special number for the man who had been one of its most important collaborators. Each one of Charles-Louis Philippe's friends, themselves collaborators on our magazine, had it in his heart to render homage to the deceased, whom we admired and loved above everyone. Jammes, who made a profession of particular liking for Philippe, into which there entered too a little of his cult for the poor and unfortunate, was one of the first notified. His homage was to appear at the head of the number and soon he sent it to me. I was staggered. A painfully scornful condescension was spread all over the first lines. The article itself was proper; but that insulting preamble formed a sort of head-piece, that appeared to be unpublishable. I wanted to ask Jammes to remove it, as one does before a tomb. Distrustful, however, of my own feelings, and fearing to bring in an exaggerated touchiness of friendship, I ran to find Arthur Fontaine, to show him Jammes' manuscript, ask his advice and counsel, knowing his close connection with Jammes, and that Jammes would be ready to listen to him. But Fontaine knew Jammes even better than I. And although he was just as affected as I by that incongruous manifestation, he communicated to me his fears that Jammes would refuse to change anything in his text. As a matter of fact, I received from Jammes, shortly afterwards, a telegram withdrawing his contribution, rather than change a single word of it. Jammes' prose was replaced to advantage by an admirable poem of Claudel's that we received at the last minute.

Jammes' attitude was very painful to me, to such a degree that my friendship for him was cooled off considerably by it. It was very lively at that time, although I have never been able to take him entirely seriously; and I knew how wounding and cruel certain uncompromising manifestations of his humor could be. I was not the only one of his friends to suffer from it. "I have just received a letter from Jammes," Raymond Bonheur wrote me one day, "which will be one of the sorrows of my life."

More capable of pity or of compassion, if you wish, than of real sympathy, Jammes was too full of his own importance to be able to understand anyone else. And I am not sure he understood himself very well, or that he did not invent himself a little; the most evident impulse of his heart, I mean the one that brought him out the most, was not always the most natural, or at least the most spontaneous. One day when we were taking a walk together, we surprised a little hare down in a ditch. At first Jammes, instinctively, raised his cane to kill it; but almost at once, collecting himself, composing himself:

"Oh, the poor little thing. He'll have to be taken off the road; he might get hurt."

For the great love he professed for animals often

gave way to the instinct of the huntsman; that was one of the contradictions of his nature, which, without his suspecting it, made his richness, and fed his poetry. (Like the secret debate between piety and sensuality.) In the little garden of his first house at Orthez, where I had been to pass a few days with him, a puff of wind brought to us the odor of burned powder, like what one smells after fireworks or shots. Anybody else would have thought, doubtless: "Why, that smells like powder." Jammes exclaimed:

"That smells like game."

I remember that remark was later the joy of Jacques Rivière. He saw in it one of those subconscious leaps of the mind, the most character-revealing, and I think he was right.

Jammes readily confused with kindness, a sort of nervous sensibility, which certainly disposes one toward it, but does not necessarily lead one to abnegation.

At Biskra, on a certain evening when we had been visiting the Negro village, we were attracted by the cries and laughter of a group of children who were frisking about on the square. Having approached, we saw they were amusing themselves with the vain efforts to fly that an unfortunate sparrow, held back by a string on its foot, was making. We wanted to free the bird at once, and bought it from the children. Jammes, standing a little apart, pretended, in order to reassure my wife, to give the bird its liberty; but coming up to me, he whispered:

"I have him in my pocket. He can not fly. Don't tell Madame Gide. I am trying to strangle him. . . . I feel him struggling. Ah! How it hurts me! It is horrible!"

That trip in Algeria had taken Jammes as far as Touggourt and it was there he left us to go back to Orthez as quickly as possible. We had made the long trip from Biskra to Touggourt in the stage. We were accompanied by Athman, from whom Jammes had just composed this short fragment that, moreover, I have quoted elsewhere:

My dear friend Athman
the trees that bear almonds
the fig-trees and black currants
are to be seated
under when fatigue is great.

One remains without moving at all
on closing one's eyes.
One is lazily happy.
The garden, one hears below
limpid water that sings
like an Arab woman.

One is so comfortable lazy
on closing one's eyes
as if one were asleep,

one is so comfortable, Athman,
that one thinks he is dead.

Jammes made fun of him; he explained our proverbs to him, and what the following meant: "Un bon tiens vaut mieux que deux tu l'auras."[1]

"The *tulores,*" he told him, "are a sort of fat trombone from which can be gotten only frightful sounds. The *tiens* is a kind of little flute. . . ."

Athman couldn't stop laughing and lent himself to the game.

It was in memory of this trip that Jammes later made me a present of an extraordinary cane. He had gotten it himself, I believe, from an old shepherd in the Pyrenean foot-hills. Cut from an extremely hard wood, it ended in a dog's head, roughly carved. Jammes had carved on it with a knife, in capital letters, the following lines:

A bee sleeps
On the heather of my heart.

A squirrel had a
Rose in its mouth. A donkey
Treated him like a fool.

A nightingale loved a wasp
He ate her with a kiss.

[1] "A bird in the hand is worth two in the bush." Literal translation: *"One good thing you have is worth more than two things you will have."* Translator's note.

The first two lines appear as an epigraph printed at the head of his letters of 1894.

I have guarded the cane preciously. It is there in the corner of my room. I can not see it without reliving the past. It helps me bring back to life a figure who was dear to me, a friend whom I have never entirely lost.

9

THE RADIANCE OF PAUL VALÉRY

PAUL VALÉRY's death does not grieve France alone; from the entire world goes up the lamentation of all those whom his voice could reach. The work remains, it is true, as immortal as a human work can claim to be, and one whose radiance will continue to spread out across space and time. I leave to others the care of eulogizing this imposing work, capable of instructing and fertilizing the most distant minds and the most diverse; that prose and verse of a severity, plenitude and beauty so perfect that they force admiration and can be compared only to the purest jewels of our literature. It is of the man himself I would speak; of what Paul Valéry was. In him I am losing my oldest friend. A friendship of more than fifty years, without lapses, clashes or breaks and, such, in a word, as doubtless we deserved, different as we were from each other. Even though confessions were distasteful to him and he held the particular and individual in considerable scorn, without doubt he would pardon me for permitting to-day the expression of my personal grief. Since he considered that, as a general thing, he should reveal only his thought to the world, many people found it possible to misunderstand him, and see in him only a prodigious intelligence, bringing everything and everybody into action without committing or permitting himself to be moved or touched by anything. . . . His reticence in regard to his sentiments was extreme, and his reserve; to such an extent that he himself scarcely seemed to suspect what his exquisite sensibility, what the qualities of his heart contributed in the way of secret quivering even in his most noble lines. And it was also those qualities of heart, that affectionate attention, even at times that tenderness, which made Valéry's friendship so precious. As for the rest, that intellectual treasure, I shall find all that again in his books; but his smile, so affectionate as soon as he had ceased to be ironical, his look, certain inflections of his voice, almost caressing, well, all that is nothing more now than a memory.

At the beginning of May 1942, on the point of embarking for Tunis, I had the joy of seeing Valéry again; he had come to join me at Marseilles. He who, so often, in Paris, weighed down by cares, duties and obligations, gave evidence of a painful fatigue, appeared to me, during those two days of sun and holiday we spent together, rested, as though rejuvenated, in full possession of his worth, more alive, more loving, more expansive than in the best times of his youth. An extraordinary gaiety animated his eloquent remarks, and I remained dazzled by the resources of his intelligence, charmed by his ease and affectionate grace.

When, after my three years' exile in North Africa, I was finally able to reach France, I found Paul Valéry again, older than I had allowed myself to expect. "I am at the end of my rope," he said to me, secretly attacked by the disease that soon became evident. Stomach ulcers, hemorrhages, pulmonary congestion . . . for a month in bed, penicillin, blood transfusions; the most constant care of those nearest to him only succeeded in prolonging the atrocious pains. The few times I was able to see him again, the suffering imprinted on his features made him almost unrecognizable. At the time of my next to the last visit, he kept me a long time at his bedside, one of my hands held tightly between both of his, as though he expected from that contact a sort of mystical transfusion. He made an effort to speak to me and, for a long time leaning over him, I made an effort to understand him, but could not, alas! get anything from his mouth but indistinct words. He had, nevertheless, kept his perfect presence of mind; and a few days sooner, was still taking some pleasure, some comfort at least, in reading; a huge bound volume lay on his bed; it was Voltaire's *Essay on the Spirit and Customs of Nations;* of that Voltaire of whom he said, at the Sorbonne, the 10th of December, 1944: "He is the man of highest intelligence, the most subtle of humans, the most ready, the most awake . . . possessing, up to the last day, springs of reactivity seemingly inexhaustible." Did he think as he wrote this that those words could be just as well applied to him?

I still read in that very last lecture of Valéry's these sentences in which, painting Voltaire, he paints himself: "Everything excites his desires to know, to reduce, to combat; everything is food for him and serves to feed that fire, so clear, so bright, where a perpetual transmutation is at work . . . where the genius of disassociation resolves every appearance of truth that drags on into the century and which still imposes itself on the indolence of the minds."

O least indolent of beings! you, animated, both by that "genius of disassociation," and by a splendid poetic genius that did not visit Voltaire at all, you fought ceaselessly with the loyal arms of the Mind alone, for durable and pacific victories. While shadows besiege us on all sides, through you France spreads a radiance over the world; and what you bring to the world can not be taken from us.

10

PAUL VALÉRY

NOTHING could do more or better honor to our provisional government than those glorious obsequies given officially, with ceremonies worthy of the most eminent representative of the French genius, to Paul Valéry, whose radiance maintains the primacy of our country over the spiritual world in spite of our historic reverses and our misfortune.

This recognition was all the more remarkable and surprising, for the signal worth of Paul Valéry escapes popular favor. That he has been, indirectly and as though he did not wish it, of immense service to France, is something that could only be appreciated by a very small number. His activity, disinterested in public affairs, exercised itself in a restricted domain, indifferent to events, but where, unknown to us, our destinies play. "Events bore me," he said. "Events are the froth of things. It is the sea that interests me. It is in the sea that one fishes; it is on it that one sails; it is in it that one dives. . . ."

And no one dove deeper.

* * * *

From his youth a secret ambition activates him, of such a nature that I can not imagine a more noble one; in comparison with it, Balzac's heroes make us smile. On the secular or worldly plane, where the game is played for the latter, Valéry will succeed moreover and, furthermore, better than any of them; he knows how honors are obtained, what they are worth, and what they cost in peace of mind. He will accept the price, if it should only be to show others and to prove conclusively to himself that there is nothing there he can not attain; a matter of earning the right to scorn all that. For he has a tendency to despise everything; that is his strength. The domination he wishes is something entirely different; it is that of the mind. The rest appears laughable to him. To dominate not the mind of others but his own; to get acquainted with its functioning, make himself master of it in order to dispose of it at his will, it is to that he continuously applies his effort. Curious Narcissus; to dominate the mind by the mind. From then on the result hardly matters to him; the product, no, but the means to obtain it; when he wishes, as he wishes, to be capable of. . . . "My nature is potential," he said. It is fortunate for us that

Valéry thought he should apply his method to literary ends; now, he said: "It is in the domain of Letters I could exist the most easily." But from then on he will consider his most admirable poems, his most accomplished prose essays, as the "Q. E. D." of exercises[1]—that is how he designates his *Jeune Parque (Young Fate)*,—and as for that supreme method he applies to it, I do not doubt he would have been able to exercise it in all other fields with just as victorious results. Yes, I imagine Paul Valéry an equally great statesman, great diplomat, financier, man of science, engineer or doctor. And I happen even to doubt if he would not have been able to excel in architecture, in painting or in music, as he did in poetry, although it requires particular gifts, but ones that Valéry possessed almost equally.

Following the example of Edgar Poe, he took this as a premise: that the artist (painter, poet or musician) should count not on his own emotion, but on the one he wishes to provoke in the listener, the spectator or the reader. Just like the actor whom Diderot praises, in his *Paradox on the Comedian,* it is not a question of being moved oneself, but of moving. Both Leonardo da Vinci and Wagner proceeded that way. Valéry refuses to believe in the Muse of the Romantics, makes fun of what is called "inspiration."

[1] "I ascribe all that I think of art to the idea of exercise."

He adopted with pleasure the words of Flaubert: "Inspiration? That consists of sitting down to the table at the same time every day." Up to the very end of his life, Valéry, rising before dawn, worked until the distracting awakening of others.

He worked in Descartes' fashion, I suppose; not at first on such or such a work exactly, but in delving into the last entrenchments of his thought. For nearly twenty years, while his companions of the out-set did their utmost at productions he judged of little importance, Valéry kept silent and searched. Before every work of merit, the question came to him: how was it obtained? The dish served claimed him less than the importance of the recipe. He turned up his nose at the risky sparks of genius. And from the first he could not bear to be duped. While still very young (we were not yet twenty years old when there began between us that inestimable relationship which death alone came to interrupt), he had pinned on the wall of his room the famous precept: "Remember to distrust yourself" (I have forgotten how that is expressed in Greek). Distrust which he applied to everything, to beings, to things, to convictions, to professions of faith, above all to words, those atoms, and one knows what latent energy the decomposition of the latter sets in motion.

I recall the reading out loud he began, from some eloquent discourse or other of Barrès' (we were sitting together in a little café on the Boulevard Saint-Germain, near the ministry of war where he then occupied a very modest position as employe). Smiling he swelled out his voice, then, leaving the text, but without changing the tone and as though "linking it up," he continued to the conclusion: "And one sees rising up the spectre (a beat) of hideous facility." He held everything easy in scorn, in horror. Whence his untiring exigency toward himself, that was to take him so far. Meanwhile, he *produced* nothing.

Nevertheless his silence began to worry us. Certain colleagues spoke of it ironically: "Well! your great Valéry, so well begun! . . . He contents himself with those few youthful poems; fine promises to be sure. Now he is silent. He will always be silent. Confess you have overrated him a little. He has given out already. . . ." He was taken for a trifler, already almost a "flunker."

However, his conversation remained dazzling to such a degree that sometimes I came to fear he would satisfy himself with it. I feared also for him the lure of mathematics, in view of his love of precision. It was not before a table full of white paper that he worked then, but before an enormous blackboard, very cumbersome for the modest little room he occupied at that time.[1] He traced on it strange signs,

[1] Cul-de-sac Royer-Collard, at the foot of rue Gay-Lussac.

complicated equations of which I did not understand an iota, formulas he explained to me at length, in spite of my incompetency; for he cared very little whether he was understood or not; it was more for himself and to himself that he spoke than for others. From that the lack of care he expended on his delivery which, up to the end of his life, remained very faulty; it often happened that his flock at the College of France, at the Vieux-Colombier, at the Sorbonne or elsewhere, had to content itself with seeing him and give up understanding him, not being able, as in a private conversation, to beg him to repeat his sentences. Besides, he often contented himself with any listener at all, provided that the latter seemed to him to pay sufficient attention and to let him orate to his fill without interrupting him. In the time of our youth he sang the praises of a certain "interlocutor," deferential and silent as he could wish, who drank in his words and was satisfied to indicate his astonishment by looks; he found him anew every day at the same hour on the platform of the omnibus. This stranger intrigued me. I became jealous of him. Who could he be? . . . Checking up finally enabled me to discover that he was the swimming teacher from the Rochechouart swimming pool.

Mathematics and algebra filled his mind; not at first geometry, for which, at the beginning, he showed a determined lack of understanding: "When, for the first time, in class, I heard the professor say: 'Let us take the triangle ABC and transpose it onto the triangle A′B′C′,' my mind refused to follow."[1] What could that mean? Useless to continue: I don't get it. It will be for others to judge whether this conclusion about geometry is admissible, and I doubt that Valéry would have been able to sustain it, while pursuing intrepidly, on the other hand, the study of astronomy, for instance. He lent to Lobatchewsky, Maxwell and Riemann an attention he refused to literary works. During a stay at La Roque, where he had had the great pleasure of finding on his night-table the writings of Maxwell, that I had had the pleasure of getting to offer him, he took from my library one evening the two volumes of *Martin Chuzzlewit* by Dickens, that he returned to me the next morning, having passed a part of the night, he said, in reading them.

"What! Completely?" I exclaimed.

"Oh! . . . sufficiently. I acquainted myself with his processes which are agreeable enough. I saw his starting point and his point of arrival. Between the two, there is just stuffing. A good secretary, having once grasped his method, could have worked it out about as well. The *Fara da se* does not interest me."

---

[1] Incidentally he comes back to it again in 1934, in his essay: *Fluctuations on Liberty,* in which we read: "I can not even conceive of that equality of figures used in geometry."

He made quick work of assimilating the little nutritive matter in a book, and, as a rule, once he had seen "what it was driving at," his curiosity passed on to something else. Even if he was enchanted, he didn't care to linger. *Ars non stagnat* remained his devise; and, if he considered a work of art only in so far as the artist can do it over again at will, "why do again," he thought, "what has already been perfected?" It was important to bring every enterprise to perfection at once, in order to be able to relinquish it immediately afterwards. That is the source of his accomplished works that were each one, turn by turn, his great poems, after he had gotten his hand in with the "exercises" of *La Jeune Parque*. Ceaselessly he went forward, adhering with modesty to the concealment of his gropings, his touching-up, his sketches, and letting his colleagues all about him lag behind rewriting unflaggingly the same verses, the same books, or, without progress, their equivalents.

So he held literature in rather profound contempt, especially the novel. The truth is, he was not interested in others, at least in their capacity as persons; for he refused to feel. . . . I was going to say sympathy, but I would not like that word to be misunderstood and to have it thought that I mean he was incapable of loving; no, but rather he disliked another's thought or emotion, to encroach on his own domain by contagion. Was it not in this sense that La Rochefoucauld could write: "I am not very susceptible to pity, and I wish I were not so at all?"

Consequently, his admirations in the field of letters were rare, and more and more grudging, quickly reduced or passed by. That which he professed in the beginning of his career for Stendhal, for instance, I was astonished to see him, at the latter part of his life, smile at; he then claimed, paradoxically, to prefer Restif de la Bretonne or Casanova to him. Besides, he read very little,[1] feeling no need to call upon others in order to think.

Nevertheless, I think that his cult remained intact for Mallarmé, whom he considered a master and his predecessor on the arduous road along which he was to follow him, but only to bypass him soon, it seems to me. Besides, Valéry remained one of the most faithful of friends: "I am in love with friendship," he might have said with Montesquieu. In spite of his anti-semitism, so tender of heart and so sensitive—his intimate friends had many proofs of it—but also of such reticence that he would doubtless reproach me for speaking of it. This cynic was capable of attentions and exquisite courtesies with his relations and those to whom he was attached. Now that he is no more, I would dare to relate the follow-

[1] "I don't care for, nor have I any need of emotions," he wrote in regard to Stendhal. "I ask only that he teach me his method."

ing: a short time after the death of Mallarmé, he came to me saying: "There is talk of a monument they propose to erect. The list of subscribers will appear, as is proper, in the papers. However, Mallarmé is leaving a widow and a daughter in that apartment where we went so often and whose rent is still due; well? No one is worrying about that. I am not in a position to assume that responsibility all alone. I thought you would help me perhaps . . . but, don't tell anyone, will you?"

Financial worries dogged him all his life. He was always afraid of being short; this, added to his desire to oblige, kept him hiding from incessant demands, solicitations, requests. From this resulted his talks, his numerous prefaces: "One seems either not to understand or not to believe—and yet I have said it often enough—that my work is made up for the greatest part only of responses to demands or chance circumstances, and that without those solicitations or external necessities, it would not exist," he might write. The excess of obligations he allowed to be imposed upon him wore him out; he would have liked to throw up the game, ask mercy: "All these charming people will kill me," he said. "Do you know the epigraph that will have to be engraven on my tomb? —Here lies Paul Valéry killed by others." But one is forced to recognize that a number of his best pages were born thus of a provocation. Besides, nothing he wrote could be neglected. Drawing on a reserve pile, he scattered his treasures about in sparks. At any rate his writings, of a rare quality, were addressed only to a restricted public. His books were never best sellers. Their teaching could be understood only by the elite; and it was not even desirable that it be followed by a great number; for, like Nietzsche's, it is in danger of destroying those whom it does not strengthen.

His reputation was not long in spreading and not only in France. I do not know how the representative of the *Chartered Company,* having heard Valéry praised, had him come to London, while still young, to entrust him with a highly important work. Restrained by discretion, and in addition of a nature not very confiding, Valéry only notified a few people of this extraordinary adventure, eminently surprising in so inactive a life. And I hardly remember the story he told me, immediately on his return from London where that mysterious work kept him some weeks, the strange conditions of life to which he had to lend himself. Of the nature of the work, secretly engaged in, he did not tell us a single word. I only learned that, as soon as he arrived in England, received by a stranger whose name he never knew, he was taken to London, then set down in a sort of apartment comfortable but sealed; and, during the entire time of his stay, he was not at leisure to leave it; forbidden equally to communicate with anyone whatever. A servant, deaf and dumb, or claiming to be so, or who did not speak any common language, brought him his meals every day, went away without having opened his mouth. That almost agreeable jail did not come to an end until after Valéry had finished his task. He was immediately conducted to the port of embarkment by the same one who had brought him, and retained the remembrance of all that like a dream.

Journalists spoke of the employment he probably assumed, in 1900 and for a rather long time, at the Havas Agency. That is not exact. The truth is, that he occupied with the old Leboy, founder of the famous agency but retired at that time, the duties of private secretary, reader and adviser. A confidential post in which Valéry had complete freedom to exercise his wisdom, his competency in political, diplomatic and financial matters, the firmness of his judgments, his probity, his tact, and finally the exquisite courtesy of his manners and delicacy of his sentiments. He spoke of that old man, for whom he had conceived a deep affection, with great deference; "a sort of father Leuwen," he said, afflicted by active paralysis which did not leave him master of his movements. To those who came to see him, he said, not being able to hold out his hand which the infirmity made tremble: "Grasp my hand, I beg you."

Seated in a large armchair, he listened to the reading of the papers and the sermons of Bourdaloue (which he preferred to Bossuet's) ; but Valéry confessed to me that often he skipped pages. That lasted months, years. And he doubtless learned a great deal from that wise old man, in those delicate functions which put on trial the practical qualities of his mind. Leaving the abstract field of mathematics, when he brought "his eyes down to the present world," his judgments, his predictions were of a pertinence that to-day appears to us prophetic, and I do not think anyone, at that time, uttered better thought-out appreciations on the situation in Europe and France.

What he wrote in 1927 on the subject of the French nation remains astonishingly present-day and of a striking timeliness:

"This nation, nervous and full of contrasts, finds in its contrasts unexpected resources. The secret of its prodigious resistance lies, perhaps, in the great and multiple differences it combines in itself. In the French, the apparent lightness of character is accompanied by a singular endurance and elasticity. The general ease and graciousness of their relationships is joined, with them, to a sentiment critical and always wide-awake. Perhaps France is the only country in which ridicule has played an historic role; it has undermined, destroyed some regimes, and one "wise crack" is sufficient, a happy witticism (and sometimes too happy) to destroy, in the public mind, in a few moments, great powers and situations. *Moreover one observes in the French a certain natural lack of discipline which gives in always to the evidence of the necessity of discipline. It happens that one finds the nation suddenly united when one could expect to find it divided."*

Before entering into the silence, Valéry had let appear, one after the other, *The Method of Leonardo da Vinci* (1894), in the *Nouvelle Revue* of Madame Adam, and in *Le Centaure,* then directed by Pierre Louys, the amazing *M. Teste* (1895), extraordinary creation, without its like in any language; an accomplished work, perfect, before which we all had to bow our heads. As he had just revealed his method to us, through Leonardo da Vinci, Valéry gave to us here, thanks to that sort of semi-mystical alibi, his ethics, his behavior as regards things, beings, ideas and life. He held to it, and remained faithful to it up to the end, constant to himself; so that, a short time before his death, he could say (these are his own words I quote): "The principal themes about which I have grouped my thought for fifty years remain for me UNSHAKABLE." He pronounced the last word strongly accenting each syllable.

However, don't let's be deceived. Monsieur Teste is not Valéry, but just a projection of him: of a

Valéry divested of that sprightliness, that poetic humor, that pleasing graciousness, of everything that made us love him. To be sure, he was able to look upon the bustle all about as vain, and to lend it only a passing attention, but it was generally with a kind of indulgence, as long as he did not find himself disturbed by it, or even with that sort of amusement we assume sometimes in regard to the trifling games of children. I see him, at the time, manipulating for the pleasure of his intimates and with an astonishing zest, the marionettes of a little Punch and Judy theatre just as later he could lend himself to the tournaments of society conversation and the comedy of the salons. Besides he even liked to do it, received with open arms as he was, fussed over, listening little and talking a great deal, sparkling and manifestly amused to carry away such easy success, or rather to verify the ease with which success is obtained. Even with his intimate friends, the seriousness of his thought never cast a shadow over his smiling graciousness. Nothing more instructive on this point than the letter supposedly from Madame Teste, a unique text, of exquisite delicacy, and singularly revealing of the secret sensibility of that mathematician. "I think he has too much continuity in his ideas," he will make Madame Teste say a little plaintively, speaking of her terrible husband. And besides (Orientem versus) Valéry, fully conscious of the mortifying danger of a too unyielding severity, will write: "I am impatient with vague things. In them you have a sort of disease, a particular irritation, which is directed against life, for life would be impossible without 'approximately'."

It is true: it is around *approximately* that literature spreads out, in *approximately* that we all flounder. I was all too cognizant of it in his presence, and his graciousness often did not keep me from feeling embarrassed. Out of great respect for others, as well as through indifference, he tolerated religious sentiments, but only in others, refusing acceptance, needless to say, of any credo whatever. He held in particular aversion Protestantism, which divests the Christian service of everything attractive that Catholicism adds to its appearance, everything politic in its regulations, and practical in its relationships; with the result, too, that he took sides with the Jesuits against Pascal. Moreover, he evinced great scorn for pious vocabulary, as also for all vague terms: those promissory notes with no cover were discredited in his mind. In this regard, this memory, an example of the pleasing verve that I just mentioned:

Some illness or other kept me in bed several days with a fever. He came to my bedside; we talked a long time. What did we talk about? The Christian virtues, I believe, and, as I was rising to their defense, the word *abnegation* having escaped me, there was Paul jumping up, leaping from his seat, rushing toward the hall door in an assumed frenzy:

"Ice! Bring some ice, quick! . . . The invalid is raving! He ABNEGATES!"

Full of deference for others; I did not say reverence. Deference is a first and convenient step along the road of veneration which, itself, implies respect, and Valéry knew how much respect restrains us. "The white man possesses a characteristic which has caused him to advance: disrespect," writes Henri Michaux disrespectfully. Valéry, whose mind wished to "advance," did not allow himself to be stopped by any form of sloth. He said jokingly (did he write it?): "Odd how many people lose their lives in accidents because they won't let go of their umbrellas!" To get rid of every obstacle was his constant preoccupation, and a more liberated manner of thinking than his can not be imagined.

One must not reproach me, as has often been done in the case of Dostoyefsky, Goethe or Montaigne, of drawing on Valéry. Nothing more different than our two natures, more opposed than the tendencies of our two minds: mine "naturally inclined to veneration," as Goethe said of his, while Valéry's endeavored to be impious, showed itself blunt in respect to every belief admitted and uncontrolled, resolutely sceptic (at the same time doubter and searcher), not worrying about approval, approbation, sympathy, and seemingly freed of all human weaknesses, vain curiosity, casual preoccupations, lagging and shilly-shallying. To everything that might have distracted him from his quest, he said "No." While, if I lost faith, in his train and like him, it was above all in myself. He seemed scarcely conscious of his ascendancy; my friendship underwent it, not without refractoriness sometimes, but the little resistance that I tried to put up, beat a hasty retreat, was routed. One thing that appeared to me, that I never doubted, was that he was always right. I suffered from his scorn, from some of it at least, but acknowledged its justification and his right to scorn, a right acquired by force of arms. His candid iconoclastic hammer spared nothing. And at that time, I didn't know how to respond ironically to his quips, as I did a short time before the war, at the committee meeting on the radio where I had the great pleasure of having him for my neighbor at the green table; when leaning toward me (in regard to some utterance or other; the name of Homer had just been pronounced), he murmured:

"Do you know anything more boring than the *Iliad?*"

"Yes, the Chanson de Roland," I exclaimed. (Had I been more skillful, I would have answered: *La Jeune Parque.*)

Not that I took him any less seriously in those latter days (I should be tempted to say: to the contrary), but I myself had gained more assurance. In the early days to which my memories go back, I usually came out of my conversations with Paul Valéry, mind and heart upset. "He breaks your spirit with a word, and I see myself like a defective vase that the potter throws into the discard," Madame Teste wrote of her husband. Yes, that's just what I felt. She added: "He is hard as an angel," and again: "His existence seems to weaken all the others." My admiration for him had to be very lively not to permit my friendship to suffer too much from it. Nothing that I lived for seemed to have any value in his eyes, and I had doubts as to his having any consideration whatever for anything I had written or wished to write. To see in that any lack on his part would have seemed presumption on mine. But he knew how to show his affection in a manner, very discreet and almost tender, that went to my heart more surely than effusions. His confidence in my taste as a critic, when he called me into consultation for some poem he had just thought out . . . nothing could flatter or touch me more, make me understand better that he at least took into account my judgment. To be sure, confidences revolted him and, considering every confession as unhealthy exhibitionism, he had no liking at all for what pleased me and what I thought I should write; but he thought I knew how to write, and that esteem was enough for me.[1]

I was greatly surprised, one day, by his unexpected praise of one of my short articles to which I confess I attached little importance: *A Dialogue with a German,* written a short time after the other war.

"But that is only a report," I protested.

"Never mind," he said. "It is a perfect sketch."

I verily believe it is the only praise he ever addressed to me. May his portrait that I am now trying to sketch be one that would have pleased him.

However admirable the greater part of Valéry's poems appear to us, I still doubt that I prefer them to his prose; a number of his pages will remain, I believe, among the most perfect that have been written in any language. Let us add at once that I know few examples of French writers, if I can even find one (in Germany, one could mention Goethe), who have excelled equally in the two classes. And it is certainly from his prose that he has inclined the poetry of certain poets in his direction, invited a number of apprentices to write like him. This blow with the rod deserved to be given, on its encounter with excesses of license; but it is on another plane, more secret, that the extraordinary benefit of his influence is being exercised. That *asper contemptor*

---

[1] I am not speaking here of the Valéry of early years, but of the one he had become, the one he had made himself become.

deum appears to me before everything and especially as a liberating master. No one has done more than he, not even Voltaire, to emancipate us and wean us away from faiths, cults and beliefs. At the very time that a wounded France seems ready to look for consolation, refuge and salvation in devotion (as she did at the end of the reign of Louis XIV, after the reverses of our armies), the virile teaching of Valéry takes on a particular importance; so also the example of his resistance in regard to the worst acceptances. Obstinately he said "NO" and remained a living witness to the insubordination of the mind.

"How does it happen," he said to me, "that men take their rest so quickly? Why are they content with so little?"

11

HENRI GHÉON

NO, there was no break between us. Only we had stopped seeing each other. That constant companion of my life and thoughts had, as you know, been "converted" during the last war. Henceforth he walked in the shadow of the Cross, where I would not let myself follow him. God confiscated him from me. I no longer tried to turn him aside from his new path which I agreed, through friendship, to be divergent from mine. As a sceptic, I would have been able to continue the dialogue; but we were both of us in earnest, and could not, after having lived for twenty years in intimate fellowship, satisfy ourselves with relations into which nothing of our real selves entered.

His religious fervor filled him to overflowing. He lived henceforth

with the vision of God under his eyelid

in company with the saints whom he evoked in his

plays. I missed him terribly. I suffered, too, on seeing him in his superabundant literary production, content himself more and more easily, and the excellence of his intentions too often satisfy his slightest exigency. I am told that he realized it and suffered from it himself in the latter days of his life, having slowly descended, because of too much obligingness and renunciation, from the summit attained in *Sainte Cécile* and *Le Pauvre sous l'Escalier.*

I can not speak of what became of him but only of what he was at the time of perfect agreement between us: all joy, youth, enthusiasm, giving and surrender. He cast over the outer world an ecstatic glance in a sort of panicky devotion, all his senses awake, wedding each harmony, amusing himself like a child or a faun, infatuated with sympathy. "Some of everything. A great deal of it. Twice," was his device. He laughed at it with intoxication. I relished his judgment, too, very correct, very sure, which, in art, allowed him to fall in love only with the best and reject vehemently everything that did not satisfy his reason along with his sensibility. His critical articles were remarkable. He wrote them without trouble though with an extreme application. A continuous exchange between us put each of our appreciations to proof, and the approbation of one nourished the confidence of the other.

That was how he threw himself into life, full of

ardor and answering anyone who asked him what he intended to write: "Twelve novels; fifty plays; loads of poems, among them three epics; cart-loads of chronicles." In his conversation he retained a vehemence that, in his writings, was tempered by hidden wisdom, and I loved even the exaggerations to which his lyricism drove him, and that kind of overflowing generosity which made him continuously forget himself. That same generosity invited him later, when religious conviction became part of it, to the sacrifice of his sensuality; and I'd rather not have to say it: his art.

I have kept all of Ghéon's letters. I find a pile of them on my return to Paris. Badly catalogued, I seek to restore a little order to them and my eyes fall at once on some unusual sentences I had not remembered, I confess, for the state of mind they reveal was then of very short duration, but which seem to me to-day of revealing importance. Ghéon never dated his letters; but I had taken care to keep the envelopes, too; the stamp informs me that this letter is of July 16, 1905. It begins with a parenthesis:

(*on receiving your letter*)

A Catholic writer, you said (what the devil could I have written him?) *or rather a Catholic cured of writing. I take the road more and more each day. Up to now it is the clearest result of that lamentable story* (an allusion to a painfully sentimental outpouring). *Since Monday I have been sicker than ever. My past life has decidedly fallen into the pit, with all of the unforeseen, all the temporariness of reckless debauchery. I discovered I was faithful, capable of living only in that atmosphere of certainty and permanence. Evidently it is not love that can give me the guarantees I need in order to live, nor the ups and downs of my art. I say: down with art and down with life! . . . But where will I find a refuge? . . .*

* * * *

As strange as this letter seems to me on rereading it to-day, unique in Ghéon's correspondence (I am speaking of that predating his conversion), without precedent and without follow-ups (for almost immediately afterwards, his letters, without any allusion to that momentary weakness, show him plunged once more into the most hazardous adventure), this letter reveals a latent need that will render less surprising his conversion to Catholicism, at the time of the preceding war, following his encounter with my friend Dupouey.

After his conversion, I ceased to go with Ghéon. We could no longer understand each other. The separation did not come through me alone. He reproached in me what he called the *gratuity* of my thinking, having put his to the service of the faith. It seemed to me that all his judgments, whose soundness I had admired at first, were bent and inclined from then on. I told him so referring to an article he had just written on the claimed Christianity of Shakespeare. He retaliated in a long letter (May 9, 1920):

"*Alas! old man,*" he said to me in it, after having defended his new point of view, "*how do you expect a certain silence not to tend to come between us once for all? We no longer live on the same plane. (You won't accuse me all the same of taking advantage of you by proselyting!) Not being able to preach I remain silent. I abominate the Ghéon that I was and whom you regret; that is not much to say; I spew him up. And as for my friendship, which has never been more fraternal, how do you expect it to wish for you anything except what I consider as the greatest good, the only good, as the "one thing necessary?" So I can only pray; I do not fail to do so.*"

* * * *

Companion of perfect loyalty, the grief of our separation was on my side alone at first. I could not get along without him; I missed him all the time, and to know that he did not miss me only aggravated my grievance. That, in the last days of his life, he in his turn knew regret and went back to the past, is possible. They tell me so. Nothing in my life, and perhaps nothing in his, was equal or comparable to that first friendship.

12

EUGÈNE DABIT

IT WAS at Sebastopol that I left him after two months of daily companionship during which our friendship became closer and deeper day by day. Scarlet fever that was to get the better of his desire to live and of his hopes broke out the evening of August 17th. That day, during the course of a long automobile ride[1] we had had an uninterrupted conversation, one of the most confidential and the best; so that the last memory I keep of him is also the one that permits me to measure best the importance of his loss, which leaves me the most lively image of Eugène Dabit and fills my heart with the most bitter regrets. Our trip in the Soviet Union was drawing to a close; Sebastopol was the last stop, and already ripened by an extraordinary experience, we were dreaming only of our return, and of work.

[1] Up in the front of our automobile our interpreter, the comrade Bola, who had accompanied us faithfully from the beginning of our trip; who, soon after, was the only one authorized to go near the sick man; who, promoted to the position of nurse, showed herself perfectly devoted.

Yes, we had talked that day as we had never yet done, and as though we both had the presentiment that that conversation was to be the last. I recalled to him the desire he had often expressed to me by letter or during our encounters, that we should live together for a while far from Paris. "At Paris it is so hard to see each other," he said to me then. "One is always in a hurry. . . ." With what joy and enthusiasm he had accepted my proposition to come join me in the Soviet Union! Of my four travelling companions: Jef Last, Schriffin, Guilloux and him, whom Pierre Herbart and I had gone to meet in Leningrad, Eugène Dabit seemed by far the most vigorous, the most "unassailable," the farthest from death; but he spoke ceaselessly of death, as though through a restless need to thrust it from his thoughts. And he spoke in the same way of the war, ceaselessly; but of it like someone who knew it. What a memory of it he preserved! In a precious album where he had taken pleasure in framing with charming drawings the poems he had written in 1924, I read the following quatrains:

I was a soldier at twenty
What misery
To make war
When one is a child.

EUGÈNE DABIT

To live in a hole
Against the earth
Pursued like a fool
By the war.

I wore out my heart
At the crucified crossroads
Oh to die on the plain
At the threshold of a sordid day.

I have known all the cries
Hate
Suffering long as a week
Hunger, cold, discomfort.

All my friends have died
One after the other
In some accursèd place
Our love lies buried.

Deceased Leguel the Parisian
Masse and Guillaumin d'Amiens
Pignatel called the Marseillais
All asleep forever.

They have been thrown into a hole
Any place at all
To speak of it makes my heart quiver
Oh how cruel is death.

My God was it worth the trouble
To suffer so
Weary I return as humble and naked
As a stranger.

Without joy, without honor
Grief in my heart
My eyes burnt out
With the shedding of tears.

He had returned the preceding May to the battle field where he had lived that nightmare. He related that in the last pages he wrote [1], which Vendredi had just published, and which, that very day, he had had me read. He was not satisfied with them and wanted to do them over. My only criticism of them was a too timid writing.

What I say of Dabit's style is equally true of his life. As he never overrated himself and worried little about appearances, nothing in him disappointed you later, and a long association led you quickly to understand how much more he *had* than he seemed at first glance to promise. Since I had known him, my esteem for him had never ceased to grow; from each

[1] I learn that since then he wrote: *The Beautiful Sunday,* a tale that appeared on August 18 in the *Paris-Soir,* in which that constant haunting by death reappears, and an article written on the occasion of Gorki's death, recently published in *Regards.* The beautiful novelette of his: *Night,* published in Marianne on September 2, was written previously.

meeting, from each conversation with him, my friendship emerged deepened. I had then known him for a long time. He had timidly brought me his first manuscript, that he completed later, only with considerable effort. It was that of *Petit Louis*. As it was at that time, that writing scarcely satisfied me; but I found in it too many good points not to wish that Dabit could learn to bring them out better. I referred the manuscript still unfinished to Roger Martin du Gard who seemed to me better qualified than I to encourage and advise a personality very much like his own. I think I could not have done better and Dabit understood at once. He preserved a deep gratitude for the one who quickly became his friend. Perhaps, without Roger Martin du Gard, we would never have had *Hôtel du Nord*. Of what profit the lessons of his elder were to Dabit, Dabit himself never tired of repeating. The friendship and confidence manifested to him by Léopold Chauveau were, at that time too, of great assistance. *Hôtel du Nord,* as it finally issued from that combination of efforts, seemed to me a remarkable work. Please understand me: the book is in no way the result of collaboration. It is Dabit's alone. But I believe that, without the advice and constant support of Martin du Gard, without the encouragement of Chauveau, it would not have been what it finally became. It had considerable success. As for me, I still prefer the *Villa*

Oasis, which is talked of much less and which seems to me to have deeper significance; more disturbing too; for I feel keenly that, by its very subject matter, it is of such a nature as to embarrass certain supporters. Dabit realized it, but he was too honest to distort the truth for tendentious purposes. He reserved for himself the right to criticize; that is exactly why too, although a thorough communist at heart, he had refused to join the party. He could not refrain from judging those toward whom his love inclined him, and all the more severely as he would have liked to be able to approve them more. A wisdom like Montaigne's, or Sancho Panza's, put him on guard against fanaticisms. His devotion to the proletarian cause was all the more firm because it was not blind in any way. In the same manner he took care that friendship should not lead him into complacency. As for his critical articles in which he often gave proof of subtle wisdom, it happened that the most affectionate were also the most severe. I have seen him deeply and enduringly affected, afterwards, if the friend was wounded [1], for he had an extremely sensitive heart.

Eugène Dabit's last writings are long studies on El Greco and Velasquez, that I have never read. He was greatly attached to them because he loved Spain and because he loved painting. A painter himself, he

[1] I am thinking particularly of a report on one of Giono's books, in regard to which he had expressed certain reserves.

spoke of it competently. But he did not overrate himself, as I have said, and I have never known a painter or writer whose modesty was more sincere. Doubtless that is why he had so many friends. His smile was exquisite, reflecting a profound graciousness; a desire, a need to love. His voice was very soft, almost a whisper; in recent times, it was raised only when he spoke of the Popular Front in Spain, whose fate he took very much to heart. Every day he listened anxiously for Jef Last to translate for us the news of the situation as it was given by *Pravda*. Then our anxiety clashed with his optimism. He would not allow anyone to express the least doubt as to the final success of the government forces. But he doubtless insisted so loudly in order to protest against his own distress. . . .

I was going to say he "did not plume himself about anything"; but he did. Being an excellent swimmer, he was somewhat ticklish as to the superiority of his crawl and especially of "brasse coulée." We were proud of him; but we teased him and amused ourselves by calling to his attention that young Soviet swimmers could, nevertheless, surpass him in speed. He then countered with a smile:

"Perhaps; but as for me, I have style. . . ."

Louis Guilloux, who teased him affectionately about his plebeian accent, had, from the first days of the trip, invented a byplay to which Dabit lent himself with the greatest good nature. The fun lay in the fact that it was repeated each day. Every day as Dabit thought of his bath, he announced:

"I am going to take my bath, . . ."

Then Guilloux:

"Why do you say 'Take a bahth'?"

And Dabit, a little disturbed at first, then entering into the game:

"I did not say 'bahth.' I said 'bath' (and the *a* suddenly became light, sharp and flute-like).

But Guilloux went on:

"How did you say it?"

"I said 'bath'."[1]

Should I excuse myself for such a childish anecdote? It protests in its way against the stiffness of death.

The last time I saw Dabit, it was already from a distance (for we were not allowed to go near him), separated from him by the length of the huge room he occupied at the hotel in Sebastopol where we had put up five days before.

"I understand it's going a little better," I said to him. "The fever is down. (They had just taken his temperature. From 40.3 degrees the thermometer

---

[1] This passage is rather difficult to translate into English. The French word used is nager, pronounced by Dabit nâger, a pronunciation used by certain classes and in certain regions in France. Translator's note.

had fallen to 38.6 degrees.[1] We hoped it was the turning point.)

"Yes," he said, "it went down, but it is going up again now."

His voice was veiled as though choked by tonsillitis. But he said that without showing great concern, and I like to think that he did not realize the seriousness of his condition either. In the shadow where the closed shutters kept him, I could scarcely distinguish his face, highly colored by sun-tan and fever. A wet cloth covered his forehead. . . . But I do not wish, I am unable to see him again without his gentle, tender smile, still full of youth and joy, as he was on the preceding days; as he shows himself in the large photograph of him he had given me in 1932, which I kept in my study above the table where I am writing, side by side with that of our mutual friend Martin du Gard, so that Dabit's affectionate glance seems to welcome me when I enter that room once more.

Herbart and I had returned hurriedly from Moscow by plane, charged with the sad mission of breaking the news to his parents whose only son he was. Afraid they would learn of their loss through a notice in the papers, we had asked for and obtained the

[1] Centigrade. Translator's note

silence of the press; not a word of the sad news had as yet leaked out.

Eugène Dabit spoke to me often of his father and mother. He reproached me for not having gone to see them. In one conversation I had with him, he had made me promise to pay a visit to the *Hôtel du Nord,* on my return to Paris. That visit, alas! it was as a messenger of death I made it.

13

CHRISTIAN BECK

NEWLY debarked from Belgium, he came to find me one morning eager to consult me on the subject of some notes for a class edition of *Paludes* that he was preparing for Hachette. He was perhaps a little malicious about it, but very little; for he generally kept back his laughter and seemed to fear his own mockery as much as that of others.

I don't know how old he might have been; of such short stature that he could have been taken for a child if there had not been something very serious in his voice and something or other doctoral and settled in his appearance. His clean shaven face was dark complexioned, not sunburned but as though overcast. His features lighted up rarely and very little. His speech was extremely slow as were his gestures; it could have been said that he masticated his sentences; and anxious not to say anything he had not previously thought out, he hesitated a little before each word and only let go of all of it when he was ready.

He had read a great deal, and retained much; almost too much. However individual and deliberate might be the working of his mind, still one felt it a little weighed down by its stock of knowledge; so also his field of experiences somewhat obstructed by the constructions—the greater part half in ruins, it is true; but he had not had the time to tidy up the place sufficiently, although he applied himself to it as best he could, knowing very well that nothing is more cumbersome than a ruin.

He received nothing that he did not weigh, that he did not think out anew. Nothing was more touching than the conscientiousness, the patience and obstinacy of his mind; so fertile and of such good compost that everything he sowed or planted very quickly developed a pile of branches which he watched grow with amusement; he marvelled at their blossoms, delighted in their fruits, but took rest only for a few moments in their shade, so exigent was his zeal and so lively his curiosity.

The extreme slowness of his speech was the joy of certain collaborators of the *Mercure,* Jarry in particular, whose butt Beck immediately became. At some meeting or other when the coffee had been passed, Jarry could be heard exclaiming in his peculiar voice, in that artificial voice that spilled out the words like a machine, giving to each syllable, strong or weak, a mournful gleam and monotonous value:

"The lit tle Beck is going to poi son him self because I have put poi son in his cup."

Immediately the cup upset, for Beck was touchy, and that made him angry with himself, for he remained particularly anxious to show that he was not afraid.

I recall a certain evening in Mid-Lent. The *Mercure* staff had dined at the Taverne du Panthéon. When I entered the room reserved, the meal was ending. It was a sort of banquet. Ferdinand Hérold, with his downy beard, was giving a toast to Camille Mauclair. Jarry, who treated himself well, had, before everybody, drunk a full glass of pure absinth, with the result that we were only half reassured when he was heard announcing in his colorless voice:

"And now we are go ing to kill the lit tle Beck."

They thought, of course, it was in fun; but with old Ubu, could one ever know? Jarry pulled a revolver out of his pocket. Then Beck, brazening it out, got up on a chair and, offering himself to the bullet, assumed a Napoleonic pose. Someone had the presence of mind to turn off the switch. The shot went blind. . . . When they turned on the lights again, Christian Beck still held his pose, as though turned to stone. The pistol was charged with a blank; but one of the guests (I don't remember who) complained of having received the plug in his eye. He kept repeating:

"No, no, it's nothing . . . but jokes like that . . . it's ridiculous! . . ."

Many other things happened that evening. But let us return to Christian Beck.

Beck was always worrying about what might be thought of him, and what they could be saying about him the moment his back was turned. It was, doubtless, a weakness but so naive and admitted that it became almost amusing; he joked with me:

"I left them," he said, speaking of a literary meeting, "so as to allow them to talk about me. But I'm not sure they're doing it. . . . Perhaps I would have done better to stay," he added slowly. "Suppose I go back? What do you think? . . ."

I stopped seeing him for a while. He had fallen ill and was treating himself in Italy. I could not take this illness seriously. Tuberculosis, he said. If I knew him, he would get the best of it, that was certain. Patience, method and resolution; what more could you ask? He had them all. He was not very wealthy, but neither was he destitute, and over there, life was not dear. He invited me to come to see him at Sorrento. I did. I think he was coming from Capri. We met at Naples on the quay. I would scarcely have known him. Hadn't he grown a beard! His cordiality, easier and less studied than in Paris, was charming. He spoke to me of his health, of his reading, and of numerous projects.

The inn to which we had gone had only one double room to offer us. Beck asked me if it would disturb me to have the window left open; that was my habit, too.

"But I'm afraid of the humidity," he said.

And astounded, I saw him pick up and carry into the corridor the bucket, water pitcher and toilet pail from which the cover was missing. Alas! we were no sooner in bed than it began to pour, and did not stop all night.

The news of his death surprised me greatly and grieved me very much. His was a mind very much alive that promised to have much to say, and I didn't think it possible that he would leave us almost without having spoken.

14

ANTONIN ARTAUD

IN the back of the auditorium — of that dear old auditorium of the Vieux Colombier that could seat about three hundred persons—there were a half dozen rowdies come to the meeting in hopes of having some fun. Oh! I believe they would have gotten themselves locked up by Artaud's warm friends scattered about the auditorium. But no; after one very timid attempt at rowdyism, there was no call to interfere. . . . We were present at a stupendous spectacle; Artaud triumphed, turning mockery and insolent nonsense into respect; he dominated. . . .

I had known Artaud for a long time, both his anguish and his genius. Never before had he seemed so admirable to me. Nothing remained of his material being except expression. His great ungainly form, his face consumed by internal fire, his hands like those of a drowning man, either extended toward assistance beyond reach, or twisted in agony, or most often tightly clasped over his face, hiding and revealing it turn and turn about, everything about him disclosed the abominable human anguish, a sort of damnation without succor, without possible escape except into a wild lyricism which reached the public only in ribald, imprecatory and blasphemous outbursts. And without a doubt could be found here the marvelous actor that this artist could become. But it was his own person he was offering to the public, with a sort of shameless third rate acting, through which penetrated a total authenticity. Reason beat a retreat; not only his, but that of the whole audience, of all of us, spectators at that atrocious drama, reduced to the roles of ill-willed supernumeraries, jackasses and mere nobodies. Oh, no, no one in the audience had any more desire to laugh; and Artaud had even taken away from us, for a long time, the desire to laugh. He had forced us into his tragic game of revolt against everything that, admitted by us, remained for him, purer, inadmissable.

We are not yet born.
We are not yet in the world.
There is no world yet.
Things are not yet made.
The reason for being is not yet found. . . .

On leaving that unforgettable gathering, the public remained silent. What could they say? They had just seen an unhappy man, fearfully shaken by a god, as on the threshold of a deep grotto, secret cave of the Sybil where nothing profane is tolerated, where, as on a poetic Carmel, a *vates* exposed, offers to the thunderbolt, to the devouring vultures, at the same time both priest and victim. . . . We felt ashamed to go back to our places in a world where comfort consists of compromises.

March 1948.

15

LE MERCURE DE FRANCE[1]

THE literary group under the protection of the *Mercure de France* was certainly of considerable importance. I can testify for it but feel too ill qualified to speak of it, having never been a part of it except from the end of my pen. Then, too, I rarely went to Madame Rachilde's receptions. Just the same, I have a keen remembrance of the infrequent appearances I made in her very hospitable salon. It was in the heyday of Alfred Jarry, an unimaginable figure whom I met also at Marcel Schwob's and elsewhere, always with the most keen enjoyment, before he sank frightfully into the attacks of *delirium tremens*. This Kobold, with his painted face, accoutred like a circus clown and playing a fantastic character, constructed, resolutely artificial and beyond which nothing human manifested itself in him, exercised

1 Weekly review founded in 1672 for the publication ot novelettes, short poems and anecdoies. Discontinued in 1825. In 1890 a group of Symbolists founded a magazine of the same name for the publication of literary information. Translator's note.

on the *Mercure* (at that time) a kind of singular fascination. Everybody, almost everybody around him, tried, with more or less success, to imitate, to adopt, his humor and above all his peculiar mode of expression, implacable, without inflections or shades, with an equal accent on every syllable, including the mutes. If a nutcracker had spoken, it could not have done otherwise. He asserted himself without embarrassment, holding conventions in perfect contempt. The surrealists, later on, invented nothing better and it is with justice that they recognize him and salute in him a fore-runner. It would not have been possible to push negation further, and that in writings often harsh and durable in form; "definitive" as people liked to say yesterday; but to-day nothing is admitted to be definitive. Still more than his *Ubu Roi,* I consider Ubu's dialogues with Professor Achras and the following debate with his conscience, taken from his very unevenly written *Minutes de Sable Mémorial,* one of the most solid and remarkable pages of French prose.

Alongside of Jarry, the other frequenters of the Rachilde's salons gave the appearance, in my eyes at least, of supernumeraries. As for the most notable representatives of the symbolist movement, I preferred to meet them at their homes, and I was going to say: at liberty. Yet it must be recognized that the *Mercure,* at that time, was for them the only possible meeting-place, outside of a few salons, perhaps, and cafés. But no, decidedly, at the *Mercure,* I felt them out of place; I, too; not that I suffered from my unimportance in those places; but there was no air; I was stifling there; the atmosphere seemed to me unbreathable. I could not get interested in the remarks that were exchanged, and very little in the people, any more than they were interested in me. When the *N. R. F.* asked if they could take back *Paludes* and my *Nourritures Terrestres* under their name, there was no question even of buying back the rights; Vallette unconditionally relinquished the remaining volumes, that were stagnating and cluttering up the shelves of the unsold and unsalable. Let this be said to clear up a little any connection I might have with those connected with the *Mercure,* with the sole exception of Vallette and de Léautaud.

My esteem and affection for Vallette had already been declared on one occasion when I was bringing my contribution to a sheaf of homages. I had the pleasure of finding him, irremovable in his office, welcoming everyone with good humor and graciousness; firm in his relationships, fulfilling with devotion his functions as a perfect editor; revolted by scheming, but prodigiously skillful in defending the interests of the authors edited by him. I can not think of him without a very cordial gratitude.

I am not sure I would have liked de Léautaud for

a daily diet; but in that way, from time to time, I took in his writings and conversations with unmixed pleasure. Everything in him delighted me; and first of all: that he did not try to please me. To be natural remained his only coquetry. I loved his glance, mischievous and tender at the same time; his rich voice with its sudden outbursts, enormous gales that often broke out like a trumpet of laughter, or of sarcasm or generous indignation. I loved that kind of distinction in his bearing, his gestures, his manners, in the somewhat untidy setting. What an astonishing face! It could have been mistaken for a pastel of La Tour's or of Péronneau's, a portrait of an encyclopedist that one was astonished to see come to life, that remained a perfect anachronism in our epoch; from it his spontaneous naturalness took on more savor. I loved his lack of respect for braid, decorations and degrees, outcome of his fundamental integrity; and even his lack of comprehension, his denials, sometimes excessive, his refusals; and the sincerity of his love for certain forms of art, the exclusiveness of his taste for what was French and the soundness of that taste. I loved . . . but why put into the past what still lives? With what joy I recently found once more the de Léautaud of pre-war days, scarcely aged and as though shrunken within himself, just as much Léautaud as before the torment, one of those rare witnesses of a past of which I hope to find an abundant reflection in his *Journal,* and which seems to-day almost as far away from us as the wars of the Empire or the Revolution. Just as it was, the *Mercure* represented a force, that of the mind, which restraints could only check temporarily. It will rise again soon, rejuvenated and under a new form, as the revival of the magazine will be able to prove. That is what I heartily wish.

October 1, 1946

16

LA REVUE BLANCHE

ALTHOUGH I collaborated unremittingly with the *Revue Blanche* (where for a long time the writing of book reports fell to me), I never mingled much with the group of its colleagues and am sorry to-day to have only caught glances of various remarkable personalities among them. There is doubtless not a single painter, or writer of real value, recognized to-day, who does not owe the brothers Natanson and Félix Fénéon, unerring and subtle pilot of the ship, an ample tribute of gratitude. The *Revue Blanche* quickly became, if I may say so paradoxically, a rallying point for divergences, where all the innovators, those unsubmissive to the stereotyped, to academics, to the restraints of outworn orthodoxies, were assured of finding a warm welcome. And not only a welcome. The Revue took it upon itself to sustain them to defend them against the attacks of scandalized Philistines, and slowly, tenaciously, to impose them on the attention and consideration of the public. Whence its extraordinary importance in the literary and artistic history of our times.

But as far as I know, there was not, strictly speaking, any salon of the *Revue Blanche,* where its collaborators were assured of meeting each other weekly as those of the *Mercure,* around Vallette and Rachilde. Simple offices, a sort of editor's room, where every day and at any hour, all meetings were possible. And that is how, one evening, as I was going to carry my copy to the editor's office, I passed Valloton to whom Thadée introduced me. He was only passing by, too. The *Mercure* had just published *Livre des Masques* in which Remy de Gourmont had grouped his presentations of the most noteworthy authors of the period; and each one was preceded by a wood engraving done by Valloton. The scrupulous and worthy Swiss painter, not always being able to refer to the model, was sometimes inspired by photographs (as in my case). Before holding out his hand to me, he considered me for a few minutes, then: "Heavens, my dear Gide, I would never have recognized you from my portrait."

And then Toulouse-Lautrec, Vuillard, Bonnard, Roussel, among the painters, and among the men of letters, Mirabeau, Madrus, Paul Adam, Jarry, Charles-Louis Philippe and so many others still who were discovered, launched, protected and sustained by Fénéon, I met elsewhere.

Even of Fénéon, there is nothing left for me to say, after the masterly portrait that Jean Paulhan recently traced of him.

Of the brothers Natanson, Thadée is the one I knew best; that is to say, a little less accidentally and fleetingly than his elder brother, Alexandre, or the middle one, Alfred; but the thick beard he wore, like Tristan Bernard, put up a screen against the effusions that the smiling amenity of his face would have invited. I doubt if that beard did not half conceal a simple kindness. Nevertheless, he was sensitive to everything, curious about everything, prepared for the echo, hearing nothing with indifference. Equally in love with letters and art, admirably trained by Fénéon and by his natural instinct, his mind and heart open to all generous causes. The *Revue Blanche,* at his invitation or following him, willingly "took its stand," as one says to-day. Without being exactly a partisan, it easily took on a reddish tint, and its collaborators often assumed leadership.

Courageous *Revue Blanche!* How we need you to-day!

October 1946

17

GOETHE

FOR a long time I have wished to pay a little of my debt to Goethe. I could not find a better occasion than this anniversary.[1] Goethe's name has often dropped from my pen; but until now I have never spoken directly of that genius to whom I doubtless owe more than to any other, perhaps even than to all the others together. Yes, indeed, on speaking of him, it seems to me that to-day I am paying a debt.

I had the good fortune to meet Goethe early in life. I felt at once weaving, as though in spite of me, the bonds of a profound fraternity; and, however far from him mystical digressions have sometimes carried me, it is always with a deep satisfaction in my whole being that I let myself return to him.

I do not propose to set forth here any new aspects of his work or life. I am not so presumptuous and I think I am rendering him greater homage by simply

1 March 1, 1932.

exposing the role he played in my intellectual and moral development, in my life. That role has been considerable. More important, doubtless, than the one it could play in the lives of many Germans; more important than if I had been German myself. For, coming from further off, Goethe could bring me more. If he seems to us French less German than the other authors from beyond the Rhine, that is also because he is more generally and universally human, and it is through him that his entire race attaches itself more extensively to humanity. Yet if, through him, I communicated with humanity, it was just the same, through Germany. It is a serious mistake to claim that the benefit of a great author stops at the frontiers of his country. Probably it is only fully understood by his compatriots; but everything that they do not need to learn because it is already a part of their blood, may become, for the foreigner, of inestimable wealth. Germany which, after Lessing, Winckelmann and Herder, burst into bloom with Goethe, had less to be surprised about and, yet, perhaps less to profit from in him than France. To be sure France had had Voltaire to help her fight against religious servitude; but it was with derision that carried away in the same irony both music and poetry. They soon took back their rights with Chateaubriand and the first Romantics. Goethe's action was more lasting, erecting opposite Calvary an Olympus haunted by the Muses and resounding with the most beautiful melodies. I understood, as I read him, that man can throw off his swaddling clothes without catching cold; can reject the credulity of his childhood without being impoverished by it, and that scepticism (I mean: the spirit of research) could and should become creative. I will be excused then, I hope, if I record here my personal memories of readings that counted among the most important of my life. And, as I don't think my case is in any way exceptional, it will permit an estimate of the echo Goethe can awaken in a French mind.

It was with his Second part of *Faust* that the contact began to be made. I was still in the rhetoric class when Pierre Louys had me read (and how can I help being grateful to him for it?) for the first time the dialogue with the Centaur. Every time I have reread it since, I have heard Louys' voice, bathed in tears of admiration and tenderness, mingled with that of Faust talking of Helen:

Sie ist mein einziges Begehren!

In that splendid cry which was to sum up his ethics (I mean: Pierre Louys') however admirable it seemed to me, I could not consent to see only a restriction. Nor Goethe either, it seemed to me; for he knew very well that Chiron would not have been able to devote himself to botany, medicine and Achille's education, if he had always had Helen on his back. Goethe, too, knew how to shake his shoulders. His biography, that I read not long after in a German translation of Lewes' book, informed me on that subject; I read it with such lively interest that I can not exactly say whether, since, when I think of Goethe, it is of the work or the man himself that I am thinking. There is no example in all literature, of a more perfect fusion, and it is for that reason that his teaching is so insistent. However consecrated may be the lives of certain authors, they remain apart from their productions. With Goethe there is constant interpenetration. Every one of his poems is an act; and, reciprocally, his life looks to us like a masterpiece, one of the finest. No matter which of Goethe's pages I read, I can not forget him, as I sometimes happen to forget Shakespeare when I read *Macbeth* or *Othello*. It is not the flower alone that I admire here; but, with it, the entire plant that bears and nourishes it, and from which I can not detach it. And if I yield here to the naturalist's need, I find that too in Goethe. However intellectual he may be, Goethe never loses sight of the phenomenal world. An unwavering instinct guides him, and only lets him think, anti-mystic that he is, in accordance with the laws of the perceptible world. The instinct of the naturalist is lacking in most of our "intellectuals" to-day; and that is where, I believe, Goethe could best instruct us, but where he is the least understood, and the least heeded. And that is where, doubtless, I feel myself most like him.

I did not read, at that early period of my life, all of the Second part of *Faust,* but better yet Faust's monologue on his awakening amidst an exultant nature, those lines in which the participation of the outer world appears so active that I understood immediately, to the point of embarrassment, that up to that moment (I was eighteen years old), I had only opened my soul to God; I understood He could speak to me through my senses, if the screen of books was not interposed between nature and me, and if I permitted a direct and permanent contact, a physical communion, to be established between my being and the whole of the surrounding universe.

I also read Helen's monologue:

Bewundert viel und viel gescholten . . .

How many times I repeated those words later on, exulting in that persuasion that the admiration of another goes hand in hand with blame, that one can not deserve praise without also provoking insult, and that he does not truly love the laurel who does not also love its bitterness.

My memory of the first reading of *Torquato*

Tasso, which I made not long after, remains inseparable from Schopenhauer. *The World as Will and Idea* dug a metaphysical pit under the replies in the dialogue between the poet and the man of action. It is of no importance whether Goethe himself was conscious of that deep significance or not. Is it not the property of a perfect work of art to permit of more being seen in it than the artist planned to put into it? In that dialogue two universes confront each other; action opposes the dream and pure contemplation. . . . And I loved to find time and time again in the whole life of Goethe, those antagonisms that he maintained knowingly within him, which invited him to find satisfaction only in the struggle, and not to seek repose, not to admit there was any other than the one found in death. And it was because he knew that:

On all the summits, repose

and because he did not want repose but struggle that he preferred, to the superhuman summits of the sublime both in art and in his life, the sunny slopes where grow the grain and vine, that should nourish man and that may intoxicate him.

For nothing is more treacherously untrue of Goethe's image than the serene picture that is commonly painted of him (in France at least). That sort of superior felicity where he maintains himself impassible and smiling in a region inaccessible to storms, is not his. His Spinozism does not go so far as to try to separate him from the passions that the *Ethics* helped him to understand better. On the contrary, at first he abandons himself to all of them, knowing how to learn from them, and only seeks to free himself when he has nothing more to learn from them. His aim, if he had any other than that of simply living as fully as possible, was culture, not happiness. That is what Michel Arnaud demonstrated excellently, in the pages he published in 1900 and 1901 in l'Ermitage under the title: *The Wisdom of Goethe*. I have just reread those pages; it seems to me that no one has since written anything more reasonable on Goethe, or anything better. Doubtless the conversations I had at that time with Michel Arnaud helped me to penetrate still further into the hidden recesses of the one toward whom so many natural affinities inclined me. But is it right to speak here of influence? If I allowed myself to be taught so willingly by Goethe, it was because he taught me about myself. And if I make a pun out of the word *Recognition,* it is because I recognize him in me constantly: each thought I could have, if not born of him, at least gained confidence from him. He did not turn me from my way, and in order to meet him, I did not turn aside from myself. The reading I did from his work blazed the trail of my existence. I have come across a copy of *Dichtung und Wahrheit* in which, along the margin of the considerations on the history of the Hebrew people (Book IV) I wrote in pencil: "This whole passage admirable. I read it in the casino at Biskra on February 27, 1895" . . . And I confess that, on rereading it to-day, however fine that passage still seems to me, I don't understand very well any more what pleased me so much in it at that time. It is certain that, on that day when I felt the need of going into detail, I had a sort of revelation. Perhaps I had simply found out how to absorb new confidence from that thought so simple and so simply expressed: "Der Mensch mag sich wenden, wohim er will, er mag unternehmen, was es auch sei, stets wird er auf jenen Weg wieder zurückkehren, den ihm die Natur einmal vorgezeichnet hat."[1] Yes, it was especially that which Goethe gave to me: confidence. And, in the diary which I kept at that time, I read at about the same date: "Nothing will have given me more assurance in life than the contemplation of the great figure of Goethe." I had also to free myself from the trammels of a Puritan morality that, for a time, had been well able to stiffen me and teach me resistance, but of which I now felt only the resistance and embar-

---

[1] In whatever direction man goes and whatever he undertakes, he will always come back to the road that Nature has traced for him in advance.

rassment, with the result that, the force of resistance which it had given me I was resolved to use against that very morality. Nothing was better calculated to help me than the reading of the *Roman Elegies.* I was delighted to understand them so well. I memorized whole passages of them and recited them to myself all day long; they scanned the rapid beating on my eager heart. I never tired of wondering at the legitimacy of pleasure with the astonishment of someone who, up to that day, had stumbled everywhere against prohibitions and forbidden things. What impunity! What freedom! I was to make a part of me that tranquil and harmonious blossoming in joy. And that nothing was more powerfully opposed to the Christian ideal is what the zealous defenders of the Church did not fail to perceive. It amused me to see them deny that Goethe had talent, the gift of persuasion or eloquence, when the glorious example of his life was enough to convince me that he had not lost his way, and that only those in France could deny the splendor of his writings, who did not read them in his language, but only in a disillusioning translation. However the denial that I was not surprised to see them register in respect to Goethe, I was pleased not to note in Goethe as regards them. It was natural they should not be able to accept the ethics of Goethe. It was natural that Goethe, anxious to admit everything, to understand everything, should write in speaking of them: "It is generally clear that others have just as much right to exist in their way of life, as I in mine."[1] Thus culture accepts Catholicism as a fertile stage in humanism, of that humanism which religious faith must oppose.

Yet I confess that this forebearance of Goethe's seems to me today somewhat compromising. As long as he opens his mind and heart through great need to understand everything, it is all right; but if it is through concern for tranquillity and comfort, that is what augments accordingly, in my eyes, the cutting attitude of Nietzsche.

It is not a matter of indifference that Germany alone produced these two great representatives of humanity. Goethe was necessary for Nietzsche to raise himself, not against him, but on him. When I reread Goethe, I see Nietzsche in him already in full strength. You don't have to squeeze Faust very hard to have the superman spout out; in *The Gods, The Heroes of Wieland,* I have a presentiment of *The Birth of the Tragedy;* and lastly, in his *Prometheus* (I am not speaking only of the Ode that figures also in the volume of his Poetry, but of the little drama

[1] *French Countrysides.* (Munster: December 1792). And further on: "The farewell formula of pious and kindly Catholics was not unknown or unpleasant to me; it had often been used with me by passing acquaintances, and often, too, by priests, my friends, and I don't know why I should feel ill-will toward everyone who wishes to draw me into his sphere, the only one where, according to his conviction, one can live and die in peace, in the hope of eternal felicity." (*Ibid;* end of the paragraph).

to which, a little artificially, he later attached this monologue[1]), I learned then that nothing great was attempted by man, except in revolt against the gods. None of Goethe's work exercises my mind more deeply, and that too is because his boldness is so extreme; that is why Goethe could not make up his mind easily, and then only toward the end of his life, to publish that youthful writing. Even the Ode he attached was given to the public without his consent. Here, as though in spite of himself, Goethe joins Nietzsche, or rather precedes him. But as to the state of insubordination that he paints in his *Prometheus,* Goethe is neither able nor does he wish to maintain it; he has got to return, on leaving the region of the thunder, to a climate where his thought can blossom more comfortably. He who was to attempt in the Second part of Faust a reconciliation between Faust and God by means of a dangerous Christian symbolism, desired, in a spirit of pacifism, to reconcile even with the divinities of Olympus the Titan at first in revolt. The sentence he adds to the monologue: "Minerva tritt auf, nochmals eine Vermittelung einleitend" (Minerva arrives for a new attempt at mediation) makes it sufficiently clear. And

---

[1] To my great surprise, I met, in Germany, eminent and very cultivated men of letters, who had no knowledge or memory of that work and even denied its existence; that is the reason I am quoting at some length. It is to this *Prometheus* and not to the well-known *Pandora* that Goethe alludes in the fifteenth book of *Dichtung und Wahrheit.*

his not being able to succeed in finding a satisfactory formula for the reconciliation, or his coming to regard that reconciliation as impossible or vain, is what explains the interruption of that work about which Goethe had, nevertheless, scarcely ceased to think, for it symbolized and resumed admirably the torment of his own mind. I will say more: that peace that he attained in his life, he was doubtless only able to obtain by cheating a little; he could not consent to trickery in a work of art; so it remained incomplete.

If the harsh chastity of Nietzsche drives further a boldness more constant and not less noble, I admire and love in Goethe, companion of his strength, that loving tenderness that causes him to make Prometheus bend over Pandora:

And thou, Pandora,
Holy receptacle of all the gifts
That dispense joy
Under the distant sky
Upon an immense earth;
Everything that causes my being to exult,
That which, in the coolness of the shade,
Showers me with comfort,
And the spring-time joy of the friendly sun
And the warm waves of the Ocean,
If their tenderness has ever caressed my breast

And all that whose pure celestial glow
Has delighted my soul with repose. . . .
All that, all . . . My Pandora![1]

Even the universality of Goethe and the equilibrium in which he maintains his faculties, are not unaccompanied by a sort of moderation and temperance. Or rather; only moderation permits this happy equilibrium, against which Nietzsche soon sets his face. Dionysus triumphs here. Goethe is a little suspicious of intoxication and prefers to let Apollo dominate. His work, impregnated with rays, has none of those mysterious retreats in which to shelter his supreme agony and his gloom. He can shed gentle tears; he is never heard to sob. Nietzsche will require more of man, it is true; but the example of this thunder-struck Titan, of this Prometheus without Pandora, that indeed is our own fragility which he is recalling. To his anxious question: "What can a man do?" no one has responded better than Goethe.

---

1 Und du, Pandora
Heiliges Gefäss der Gaben alle
Die ergötzlich sind
Unter dem weiten Himmel,
Auf der unendlichen Erde,
Alles, was mich je erquickt von Wonnegefühl,
Was in der Schattens Kühle
Mir Labsal ergossen,
Der Sonne Liebe jemals Frühlingswonne,
Des Meeres Laue Welle
Jemals Zärtlichkeit an meinen Busen angeschmiegt,
Und was ich je für reinen Himmelsglanz
Und Seelenruhgenuss geschmeckt . . .
Das all all . . . Meine Pandora!

18

THE TEACHING OF POUSSIN

There, all is nought but order and beauty. BAUDELAIRE.

WHAT has been called "The Criticism of Art" is, of all the literary types, the most dangerous, and rare are the men of letters who can succeed in it, risking themselves in a terrain that is not, strictly speaking, their own. If I dare do it to-day, it is without any presumption whatever and fully conscious of the danger. For, in spite of what is said of it by Félibien, the first of those art critics, who before the end of the seventeenth century wrote: "the light of reason is above what the workman's hand can execute"—the qualifications of the trade remain of primordial importance, and the man of letters knows nothing about them.

However, of all those who "made a profession of mute things," there is not one whose works, as much as those of Poussin, extend beyond the interest in painting alone and which, for their noteworthy success, have made appeal to qualities and virtues rising far above the exclusive merits of the brush.

During Poussin's life as well as long afterwards in order to praise his canvasses, they pointed out (even men of his trade) only their intellectual merits, and discussed reasonably to their wits' end the why and wherefore of those merits. Better advised to-day, perhaps, we know that those merits, however extraordinary they might be, would not have sufficed to assure Poussin a lasting reputation, to permit his canvasses to pass into distant times and to come down to us. In the great shipwreck of time, it is by their skin that masterpieces float. The same for literature. Without the inimitable beauty of his prose, who would still be interested in Bossuet?

I shall go further: intelligence even risked holding Poussin back, as often happens. Here the miracle is that Poussin was painter enough, was a great enough painter, so that the container, under the excessive weight of what it contained, did not go under; so that the idea triumphant could dominate the matter while glorifying it. And that is because, in him an idea immediately became an image, was born plastic, and that here the intention, emotion, form, craft, everything converged on and conspired for the work of art. With the result that what Barbey d'Auvevilly wrote of Baudelaire could be said of him: "Following that struggle with the angel, the artist was not too defeated."

That Poussin is a painter, a great painter, a born painter, we would be sufficiently convinced by one of his mythological canvasses, not cluttered up with meaning, representing a naked nymph, or some sleeping Venus, and responding only to what Poussin proclaimed to be the aim of art: delight. But these canvasses in his first style, scattered over Europe, are relatively little known. Likewise, when it was granted us, at the time of a great exposition, to see in Paris a certain work of Poussin that had been lent to us: *Tancrede and Hermione* or *The Inspiration of Anacréon,* it was a dazzling revelation for many of the French. What! Poussin capable of such discreet splendor, of that gleaming, blended enamel, of that sumptuous symphony? Who would have thought it after his classic and too sober masterpieces in the Louvre?

Now, having once tasted easily that jubilation, that sensorial rapture, we shall know how to find it again even in his last canvasses, however tempered they may be by the monotonous patina, and cooled off too, accustomed as we are to them. At any rate, of less flagrant sensuality, they require of us, to be affected and to affect us, a very vigilant attention, a prolonged contemplation.

Moreover, to persuade us, there is nothing better

than those fragmentary, photographic representations—where, leaving behind the harmonious vision of the whole, we can evaluate in a leisurely way the sensibility of the touch, its firmness, its fullness; and it is with a sort of particular intoxication that we admire from then on the essentially pictorial qualities of the innovator, by which he overtakes certain of our boldest pioneers of to-day.

Let us get down to Poussin.

I don't have to expound on his biography. I shall note only that he was about eighteen when he made his first fillip at the doctrine of Barrès, at the attachment to "the land of the dead." As soon as he "thought he was in a position to leave his native region," writes Félibien in 1685, "he left his father's home (in Andelys) without making any stir, and came to Paris to learn more about an Art whose difficulties he already recognized, but which he loved passionately." And a few years later, it is France itself that he leaves for Italy. During his first trip, his means and circumstances did not permit him to go further south than Florence. But the second time, making a greater leap, in the spring of 1624, he reached Rome, where he settled down and blossomed forth. Nevertheless, an especial appeal from Louis XIII recalled him to Paris where important charges were entrusted to him, accompanied by extraordinary advantages. "Now," remarks Félibien, "whatever charms might have retained him in Italy, it would have been very awkward for him not to obey the orders his King deigned to give him" (in January 1639) . Still he only answered him with very bad grace, procrastinating until the very end of 1640, until the extreme limit of propriety. Then, as soon as he could, breaking all his engagements, he settled again in Rome (in September 1642) which he never again left until his death (November 19, 1665). The scrupulous Paul Desjardins feels justified in writing: "There is not a trace in Nicolas Poussin's letters of any obligation that he might have felt toward his parents. Never afterwards does he show any regret at being separated from them; transplanted voluntarily to Rome, he lost all desire to return, it could even be said all memory." The first of our great painters, and the most French of our great painters was the type par excellence of the uprooted person. Others are almost as much so, and among them Claude Gelée from Lorraine; but no one more advisably than he. Yet it is the spirit and genius of France that can be felt breathing in his canvasses and that he illustrates in a different way, but just as much as Descartes[1] (that other great up-rooted one) and Corneille[2], his contemporaries.

The three portraits (by himself) that we have, of

---

1 Born in 1596.
2 Born in 1606.

1622[3] and of 1630[4] present to us a Poussin dictatorial and a little grumpy. The severity of his features is not softened by any desire to charm. In the little sanguine in the British Museum[5] Poussin accentuates the disdainful twist of his lips that, as early as the portrait of 1622, one felt little made for smiling, and the frowning of his eyebrows over a sharp and inquisitorial look where, in the first portrait, can be read above all interrogation and expectation. In the celebrated and more conventional portrait in the Louvre, he attains a sort of gloomy serenity. With such a face, he can readily be imagined "young or old, always alone in his studio."[6] In spite of the great influence exercised by him, he never formed any disciples; neither had he been the pupil of any master. It might be said that something was lacking because he had not served the apprenticeship of his trade; but the very defect in his virtuosity and the slowness of his hand preserved his secret value.

Malraux affirms with wide-awake perspicacity that the first creative impulse of any painter is never given directly by nature, but by some preceding work in which nature has already been interpreted; that without Cimabué there would never have been

3 Collection of the Marchoness of Bute at Luton (Scotland).

4 Louvre.

5 "Rittrato originale simigliantissimo . . . fatto nello specchio di propria mano circa l'anno 1630, nella convalescenza della sua grave malattia. . . ." The rubric on the portrait tells us.

6 Louis Hourticq, *Poussin's Youth,* p. 45.

a Giotto; with the result that one can go back in this way to the graffito of the caves, those traced for the purposes of magic. For no painter is this determination truer than for Poussin. Most certainly the external beauty of the world did not leave him insensible, but it was in contact with works of art that he became conscious of his vocation. Self-taught, he put himself, when young, into the school of the ancients, bas-reliefs and statues, copying them in preference to animated or "still" life; then under the great Italian painters, of Raphael especially, whose works, moreover, he knew for a long time only through engraved reproductions. And just like Ingres later, he could have said: "My works recognize no other discipline than that of the ancients, the great masters of that century of glorious memory, when Raphael defined the eternal and incontestable limits of the sublime art. I think I have proved in my pictures that my only ambition is to be like them and to continue art on taking it up where they left off."

Poussin is first and foremost a *composer*. And so he almost never works from a model, giving less heed to the counsel of reality than to the instruction of the great masters; "sucking in the milk" of Raphael, his first biographers, Bellori then Félibien say later, "receiving the nourishment and the spirit of Art, as he saw it in the works." Poussin puts himself voluntarily and deliberately *in the train of*. . . . What is it then, what is there in him, that permits Delacroix, so different from him in so many respects, but such a judicious connoisseur, to consider him as "one of the boldest innovators in the history of painting?" What he adds throws light on his thought: "Poussin arrived in the midst of affected schools in which craft was preferred to the intellectual side of art. He broke with all that falsity."[1] Contrary to other painters, and I am speaking even of the greatest, he does not abandon himself to his gifts, does not give them full play. "There is no fine art without consciousness, and consciousness and the spirit of criticism are the same thing," writes Oscar Wilde. Nicolas Poussin was and is the most conscious of the painters, and that is also where he shows himself the most French. "E un pittore che labora di là," Bernin said of him, pointing to his forehead. Thought presides at the birth of every one of his pictures.

But just as Mallarmé (who was the most intellectual of the poets before Valéry) could say it is not with thoughts that one writes poetry, it is with words, Poussin teaches us: it is not with thoughts either that pictures are painted, but with lines and colors. Which does not prevent thought from coming to inhabit his canvasses, subordinate colors and lines

[1] *Essay on Poussin,* in the *Moniteur,* June-July 1853.

to it, coordinate them and bring everything into harmony.

He may appear, like Ingres, a drawer rather than a painter; and often the picture may be for him only the putting of volumes into color, for even his drawing remains grouping and composition. The sensuality of the eye may very well guide him, but will never be ruling mistress; reason enthroned will always force her to respect. Dominiquin, the only living painter Poussin did not despise and consented to listen to, said to his pupils, and Poussin likes to repeat it after him: "Not a line should come from the hand of the painter that has not first been formed in his mind."

But in advancing this delicate truth (so simple that I blush to have to express it) that, by whatever art the artist expresses himself, the craft should be only a subjugated instrument, I shall cause myself to be treated as a vandal, so unknown is it to-day; in our time, so often, that *Serva* has been made *Padron;* so often does she reign as despot, and everything else keeps silent before her.

And doubtless I can be moved, as much as by the most expressive figure, by a certain "still life" of Chardin, a dish of plums on a copper fountain, whose substantial gravity, whose devotion to art, is worthy of the meditation of Descartes; doubtless I may even prefer some little canvas of Delacroix, representing the *Interior of the Duke de Morny's Home,* I think, or a certain red-hot *iron stove,* to some pathetic composition where he falls into the declamatory. . . . I should like to be understood; what I don't like, is to hear it announced preemptorily. . . . This is *true painting* owing to its very absence of a subject; that is seeing painting divested of all spiritual virtue, so as to attach a value only to the qualities of the craft; it is seeing our greatest painters of to-day take care no longer to address themselves to our senses, to be nothing more than eye and brush. This stripping, voluntary omission, will remain, I believe, characteristic of our epoch without a hierarchy, and risks causing it to be judged severely later; yes, all the more severely because these painters will have been all the more admirable because of their craft. It is by their *lack of significance* that the paintings of our time will be recognized.

While the impressionists, of whom Monet is the most illustrious example in certain of his canvasses or succession of canvasses (I am thinking in particular of his *waterlilies* or his *haystacks*), offer us works deliberately decentralized, Seurat, and then in our times, Matisse, Picasso and still many another very important one, like to speak of composition, volume etc. . . . but the able arrangement of their canvasses remains perfectly gratuitous, independent of all subject. We have seen Matisse work for a long time on the elaboration of certain decorations, returning without respite to the modification of contours, to the skillful equilibrium of the solids. . . . Yet nothing governed their choice, except the need of filling up space. No spiritual or emotional motive. The work, in order to be real painting, was careful to mean nothing. That idea and sentiment have been deliberately banished from the plastic arts, that painting could have relinquished that immense domain of expression, which nevertheless was its own, and could be its property only, is something that will not fail to cause astonishment later on. And it will matter little if, after that, this domain is no longer inhabited except by the most mediocre painters and the most execrable works. Because he understood only too well that it is with fine sentiments and noble thoughts that the worst works of art are composed, the painter made up his mind not to express thoughts or sentiments at all any more. Moreover this "decerebrated" painting appeals to the need of an impatient public and speculating merchants. All that fits in with the "canned" age.

As I write, twenty examples come immediately to my mind, weakening my assertions. But the critic or the historian, like the painter, can not and should not take into account all the shades and all the lines; to draw is to choose. Have I drawn badly? I don't think so. In any case, it is Poussin who invited me to say all of the above; for I think if he came back to earth, that is how he would speak.

To tell the truth his ideas concern us scarcely at all and I can not make much of them. Nothing surprising or revealing in his *aphorisms* on his art, nor in his famous *Principles,* so often quoted. All that goes without saying. It is only by studying the ideas of a painter that we get them; as those of the musician, only when they come into sonorous existence. Even a poet's ideas are of value only when they fill out and animate fine poetry. Otherwise the most sublime prophecies, even of a Hugo, irritate me; I don't know what to do with them and I can't take them seriously. As for the thinker, Sully Prudhomme, I abandon him to his ruin. Poussin's idea has no value except it become plastic, and he transmit it to us pictured. But once that is said, let us recognize that it is the thought that motivates and animates all his pictures. That is what determines the grouping of his figures and their gestures, the movement of the lines, the distribution of the light, and the choice of colors. There is nothing, not even the leafing of the trees in his huge landscapes, that does not seem an emanation because of its balance and the serenity that it breathes.

And never more than in him has painting shown itself more tractable in spirit, or shown such an intention to instruct. The contemporaries of Poussin were not deceived by it; and for a long time after his death, one proved himself connoisseur in painting by explaining his pictures: not a gesture without motive, they revealed his subtle intentions; the painting was presented as a sort of picture-puzzle, for which it was necessary to find the key to be able really to admire it. After which, one would have tired of them, had their value not been, properly speaking, pictorial. Paltry teaching of a work of art, if it had had to be limited by the solution of petty problems.

The teaching I draw from it is very different. Doubtless it is Poussin's spirit speaking to me; but it is less to my mind that he speaks than to something very deep within me, that I don't know whether to call soul or will. He invites me to a very particular contemplation of nature that is only permitted to works of art, music, painting or poetry; to what Poussin himself calls "delight," the only aim, according to him, of his works. And I should like to add to that word an epithet: persuasive delight; a delight by which, as I emerge from it, my vision of the exterior world and even my demeanor recognizes itself changed.

The joy that comes to us from the contemplation of certain canvasses of Poussin is not only the delight of our senses; it is profound, durable, and the sort of serenity that I get from it ennobles me. I have only to enact the *ideas* of Poussin, I wrote; all the same, my reason too is touched here, giving consent to my joy, to the reconciliation of mind and senses in one supreme harmony.

Poussin does not search for that harmony in the expression of felicity alone; he likes to impose it in the tumult; he even obtains it in the horrible in the style of the tragic Greeks, and is not afraid to represent massacres, corpses and plague-stricken scenes. With the result that I doubt there would have been such violent aversion to Gericault's *Raft of the Medusa* as Ingres, his younger cousin, was to manifest later.

Just the same, it is the felicity in his work that carries me away, a joy sensuous and spiritual at the same time. If we find in France almost none of the mythological nudes in his first style, before the Roman gravity that he liked to paint at the time of his long sojourn in Paris, if those canvasses of a bewitching lewdness, have gone astray in museums or private galleries abroad, the reason (one of the reasons) has been given to us by his contemporary, Louis-Henri de Loménie, Count of Brienne, in a manuscript dating from about 1694, discovered and published recently by Louis Hourticq; I could not do better than quote from it, and all the more willingly since the text is little known. Speaking of Poussin, Brienne first mentions rapidly "his pictures a little too nude," *Danae, Galatea* or *The Sleeping Venus,* "and a thousand others of this nature, where the nude is a little too uncovered in view of the correctness and modesty of French manners and customs"; then, in regard to a *Venus* by Titian, he writes: This picture, although excellent, deserves to be burned, for one could not look at it . . . without emotion. I should have had it covered with a veil if it had been mine, just as I had Monsieur de Cany cover with a cloth Poussin's beautiful *Venus* that caused me so much trouble in the seminary where I am, although this picture, excellent and one that could be viewed by everyone in the state in which it now is, is nevertheless never displayed." And Brienne adds: "In the homes of the cardinals in Italy, I have seen just as nude and less chaste ones. But *in France nudes are no longer tolerated."* Painting, if not pious, or at least austere, had to be hidden.

Let us permit Louis Hourticq to assert: Poussin has "never touched on religious painting except on order and to serve the personal devotion of the giver." Neither his tastes nor his convictions led him in that direction. Others will notice too that the religious scenes he introduced into painting are among the least moving of his works; he forces himself to them.[1] In his *Jesus in the Garden of Olives,* the indiscreet introduction of cherubs, bearers of instruments of torture, takes away all solemnity from that ultra-pathetic scene, and Paul Desjardins has every reason to write: "The unreality and playfulness of that conception wound like profanity." But Poussin is not conscious of it; there is no desecration in it for him, because there is no preliminary consecration. No mystical emotion takes part in that play of the spirit. He is, and remains reasonable; cartesian, it could be said, even before the influence of Descartes began to be felt. No anxiety in him, except concerning his work; no secret torment, no appeal to redemption, no need for recourse to the supernatural, to grace.

It will be said we are not any more conscious of the religious sentiment in the religious pictures of Rubens or Van Dyck, of Titian or of Raphael who, like Poussin later, found himself fully at ease only on the Greek Parnassus, and painted with the same brush, with a serene indifference, *The School in Athenes* or *The Dispute over the Holy Sacrament.* In not one of them is there any of that inexpressible mystical emotion that illuminates the little canvas of

---

1 With the sole exception, I believe, of the *Christ wept over by the Holy Women* (not the canvass in the Pinakothek in Munich, unfortunately conventional, but the surprising picture little known, in Dublin, the only one of its kind, probably), of deep feeling and truly religious.

Rembrandt for instance; *The Disciples at Emmaus.* In any case, that assertion would be of very little importance if Poussin, like Courbet or Manet, saw and made us see nothing beyond the subject matter and had dreamed only of glorifying it. But that is not the case; don't let us be deceived by it; Poussin is an anti-realist painter; there is no one more spiritual or idealistic than he. There is not one who transports humanity more resolutely and more spontaneously at the same time, above itself. And of course I am not speaking of his *Assumption of the Virgin* or the *Rapture of Saint Paul,* in which angelic efforts cooperate. A strange thing, as to the mystical feeling of which Poussin was capable, it is in his *Inspiration of Anacreon* (or in his *Inspiration of the Poet,* although a little less perceptible) that, unexpectedly, I find it. Pagan mysticism, needless to say, but alive and sincere, and such as one would not imagine different if, instead of quenching his spiritual thirst at the cup of poetry the god holds out to him, he should slake his thirst at the communion cup. He has the gesture of offering, the ecstatic look of the communicant. And nothing is more revealing than this admirable work[1] that moves us by its extraordinary beauty, doubtless, but also like a confession.

---

[1] That the Museum of Hanover, I believe, lent to Paris at the time of the great exposition, and of which there is, at Dulwich, either a duplicate or a copy.

This inspired poet he paints (in that second picture the Louvre owns to-day) is Virgil, we may think, judging by the *Iliad* and the *Odyssey,* books that figure in the picture near the god. As Virgil imitates Homer, Poussin imitates Raphael. For his tradition forms, as though outside of time, a continuity so homogeneous that he does not hesitate to locate, in his *Orpheus* and *Eurydice,* the drama that separates the two lovers in the Greek fable, in a Roman setting where we are astounded to find the Castle of Saint-Angelus. Yes, Poussin imitates, and La Fontaine, and Racine, and Molière; and in our day, Péguy, Claudel and Valéry. And it is well to say that at a time when nothing discredits an artist more than his resemblances. It is commonly judged today that an artist has all the more value if he has risen up, invented himself out of whole cloth, and if one can no longer recognize kinships in him. But then he is in danger of rendering obeisance to the times, and in that apparent and forced originality, to yield to the anarchistic taste of the day. As far as I am concerned, I think the courageous artist is the one who bucks the current, whether it tries to carry him to the right or the left. It was by retaining and restoring tradition, when it was slipping away, that Poussin was able to seem to Delacroix healthily revolutionary. Yet his originality remains profound, but is revealed only after a thorough examination. Proud in the midst of his epoch, modest as regards the past, he wishes to be an important mile-post in a glorious culture. To attain it, he will rely only on himself, and expect it only from himself; but he will know how "to neglect nothing." It is to his own "generosity" alone that he appeals (I am quoting his own words) to maintain himself from then on in his "assured and constant position."

Félibien congratulated France for having been able to produce "so rare a man" for her own glorification, and we can only profit by putting ourselves in his school in our turn.

I take Poussin for myself?—No, not at all; it is he who takes me. It is for him to speak. I remain silent.

19

LAUTRÉAMONT

I CONSIDER that the best claim to reputation of the group formed by Breton, Aragon and Soupault, is their having recognized and proclaimed the literary and ultra-literary importance of the astonishing Lautréamont. Nothing could flatter me more than the request they made me to write a preface for the new edition of *Chants de Maldoror* they are preparing. If I declined that *honor,* it was because I considered it impertinent to explain, even to present, that work to a public with which it had nothing to do, and to bring up a stool to reach it, when it could only be obtained by a bound.

After all, it does not seem to me that Lautréamont was entirely responsible; but his strange and unprecedented power in our literature, comes, as it happens, from his knowing how to protect himself and to maintain within him that state of irresponsibility. His influence in the nineteenth century was negligible, but he is, with Rimbaud, more than Rimbaud, perhaps, the master of the sluice gates for the literature of to-morrow.

20

ARTHUR RIMBAUD[1]

I RECALL the time already far distant (it must have been in 1891) when Paul Valéry, whom I had the pleasure of coming across once more at Montpellier, said to me: "In fifty years statues will be raised to him." It was of Rimbaud he was speaking.

Statues in public places seem to me to be merited only by those who render to the public services of a nature that the public can easily appreciate: a Pasteur, an Edison, a Curie. But doubtless Valéry, when he spoke of "statues," was thinking of monuments like the one, entirely immaterial, in which you propose to group our homages in your magazine. Never mind! That prediction seems risky to me. Not that my admiration for Rimbaud was not, even at that time, most lively; but the devotion I offered him remained of a secret nature, and I could imagine only

[1] Published in *Poésie 41,* No. 6 (1941) in answer to a research article in that magazine, entitled "Arthur Rimbaud died fifty years ago."

with difficulty one ever rallying around him a number of minds of very diverse formation and tendencies. The idea of esoterism and the *happy few* is one of those to which the issue has given the most unexpected denials. Already for Stendhal and Baudelaire, as a little later for Emily Brontë, Mallarmé, Verlaine and Rimbaud, as to-day for Joyce, Melville, Proust or Péguy, the *happy few* of yesterday, are called, from now on, the multitude. That is what tempts us to think that real genius always finds its recompense; although the clear echo of its voice is sometimes awaited for a long time, and it is the case with certain poets as with those distant stars whose light reaches us only a long time after the star is dead. . . .

There is something else: Rimbaud appeared to me like a demoniacal poet, a poet "accursed" above everyone and liking to be so. The burning alcohol, the "famous swallow of poison," he invites us to drink, and that I have tasted with delectation, more heady, more exciting than any wine, could suit, I thought, only the strong. Into what strange damnation was he not leading all the others? I needed only the high authority of Claudel to assure me. Not so much on account of the saying: *omnia munda mundis,* to the pure all things are pure, but rather because of the word of Scripture: *Et violenti rapiunt illud* . . . although I don't know any too well whether

I should not apply it to Claudel himself rather than to Rimbaud: "And the forceful take possession of it. . . ." But the Catholic who takes possession of Rimbaud, with his aggravated individualism, his recalcitrance, his revolts, strongly recall to me the Spartan, whose prowess was related to us in school: he has to bear the bites of the stolen fox that he hugs to him under his gown. Rimbaud's are cruel, almost as much so as his kisses.

And this fox, in its turn, recalls to me Faust's *Pudel*: behold him increasing, becoming enormous! In the infernal shades, his eyes gleam, throw out disturbing sparks. Rimbaud does not allow himself to be put on the leash easily, even by a Claudel. The yappings of this fox partake of the roars of the wild beast. He is frightening, even when tamed; and many of those who admit him to-day would not have received him into their privacy without his mahout to guarantee to us that his intentions are, in the last analysis, praiseworthy. One might have been permitted to doubt it.

But it matters very little what such and such a person wishes to see in Rimbaud. Is it not the property of a true poetic genius to answer widely divergent questions, to lend himself to many a contradictory interpretation, to encourage disagreement in respect to him, to offer more than appears at first glance, with the result that, with him one can not stop anywhere? There is what he wished to say, what one thinks he wanted to say, but the most important, doubtless, remains what he said without wishing to and in spite of himself.

Then, in spite of double meanings which, in one sense or another, invite us to make use of him tendenciously, Rimbaud remains an amazing master of the art of writing, an inventor of forms whose newness his numberless imitators have not been able to tarnish. Now, we know that questions of form are of the highest importance, in art as well, alas, as in religion. On this ground we are agreed.

Where I go along with you less, dear Seghers, is where you claim to look for, and perhaps find, in Rimbaud a possible rallying point for our desires, for our "dreams," for our thoughts. Indeed I feel that your sentence remains prudently interrogative and that you have the honesty not to force our answers. Immediately after, you speak of French *diversity*. Recognize the danger then: if the being (and, in this case, the writer) about whom you consider it desirable for us to assemble, is simple and changeless, as Voltaire or Bossuet, I mean, if his tendency is clearly marked, he will be recognized as master by those alone possessing minds with the same tendency as his. If he is complex, "wavering and diverse" enough to give us (or permit us to take) the wrong scent, he will be able, all by himself, to represent

"French diversity," but the danger will be great that agreement on him be established by the aid of a misunderstanding.

Even "our" Péguy, that little soldier with a great heart, well-intentioned, yet simple, but uppity, humble before God alone, but in conflict with men, and protesting against authority, I am by no means certain that he would recognize as "one of his" a large number of those who claim him at present. If he were still living, that Dreyfusist, that fervent Christian who went beyond the sacraments, that fighter against orthodoxies, what would he say at seeing himself adopted by so many of the faithful who retain only that part of him that suits them? . . . And as for Rimbaud, what part of him will they retain, without all the rest of his being protesting? Will you take into account only the work of his youth, full of refractoriness, an appetite for freedom, risk and adventure, of blasphemy, and of greediness for forbidden fruit? Shall we forget the frightful bankruptcy of his life, the "ferocious invalid back from warm climes," the "motionless stump" that this "tipsy" ship became? Or shall we say that this bankruptcy was, as a matter of fact, necessary, and those disappointments in order to obtain from him finally that questionable conversion *in extremis* which just the same permits the Catholics to claim him as their own? But then what do you admire in him? His early works interrupted almost immediately, or the forgetfulness of that work, and the existence that repudiates it?

I think, in the present troublesome times (when it is important at one and the same time to repudiate none of our heritage, and to render all that patrimony, like ourselves and our wills, serviceable to the uncertain future of France), that the exaggerated individualism taught us by Rimbaud, that incomparable ferment, must be held in reserve, and that it would be as imprudent to suppress it as to accord it free rein to-day.

21

THREE MEETINGS WITH VERLAINE

I MET Verlaine three times. The first time was in January 1890. I have not a very chronological memory and, if I can give the exact date, it is because I put down that visit in my *Journal.* I was with Pierre Louys. We had both just finished the rhetoric class. I needed a leader and I believe firmly that without Louys I would never have dared to present myself either at the home of Mallarmé or of Heredia, with whom I associated a great deal after that. Louys even wanted to take me to Théodore de Banville's one day. He had just died. Pierre Louys was reproaching himself for never having gone near him. "It is a unique occasion and the last," he said to me. "Anyone is admitted." To-day I am sorry I did not see Banville on his mortuary couch. But that funereal visit ("by devotion," insisted Louys) at that time appeared to me ghoulish impropriety. I refused. But I was glad to accept when he suggested that we both go pay our respects to Verlaine at the hospital.

Our pilgrimage to Broussais is recounted by Pierre Louys with perfect fidelity in a few pages published some time ago by *Vers et Prose,* the excellent magazine directed at that time by Paul Fort. Has that little writing ever been reprinted? I doubt it. Yet it deserves to be, and I could not add anything to it.

It was Pierre Louys, too, whom I accompanied to that famous banquet in celebration of his *Passionate Pilgrim,* of which André Billy had recently spoken highly in the *Figaro.* Pierre Louys had already been initiated while I still remained awkward and timid; several very beautiful sonnets had caused him to be received warmly by Heredia and the group of poets that thronged his gatherings every Tuesday. Henri de Régnier was the most important to them, and it was to him first that Pierre Louys introduced me the evening of the banquet. The author of *Tel qu'en Songe (As in a Dream)* was courteous and distant, very self-conscious, very careful of his remarks, but of charming amenity. After the banquet, Régnier took Louys and me to the Café Voltaire, on the Place de l'Odéon, and that was where I saw Verlaine for the second time.

It was late and Verlaine was drunk. Besides he could be so at any hour of the day or night. We were already in the café when he entered abruptly, flanked by Casals, his faithful companion. Wrapped in a huge greatcoat, he seemed enormous. We were all standing. He approached Régnier and seizing him by the vest or the tie, on putting his face very close to his: "As for you, my little one, I recognize you. You are Henri de Régnier." To be sure it was a rare honor to be recognized by Verlaine; but Régnier, so lordly and perfect in his manners, seemed a little embarrassed by that drunken familiarity and the sudden use of *tu;* he put his back up and drew back a little, yet without ceasing to smile, flattered just the same, but careful to maintain a short distance between them. . . . And then Verlaine must have smelled horribly of wine. He did not say anything else to us that evening. Leaving Régnier, leaving that world, he went and slumped down in a corner, his look wandering.

My third encounter . . .

But before relating it, I should like to forestall any misunderstanding. My admiration for Verlaine is most lively. I consider him one of our greatest poets; the music of his poetry one of the most perfect and the purest that has ever been heard in France. I admire Verlaine, not *on account* of his intemperance, his habits and his irregular life; but not *in spite* of them, either. . . . I am not able, nor do I wish to dissociate one from the other. It was in the depths of the worst abasement that he found his sweetest accents, and doubtless the one was necessary to obtain the other "in a parallel direction." So I consider that I in no way minimize him by my story; to the contrary.

A few years later, I was walking one morning near Saint-Etienne-du-Mont. I had completed my first studies at the Lycée Henri IV, and the memory of the bell of that little church that, on going to the lycée and returning from it, I used to see four times a day, in all weathers, tempers the unpleasant memories I have of my class in philosophy in spite of two remarkable pupils. And so once more that day I walked around the Panthéon. It was a little after the time classes dismissed at the lycée. Some children were lingering about and my attention was attracted by a considerable group of them; about twenty very lively ones were forming a circle and frolicking about noisily. Just imagine it; they were booing a drunkard. And what a drunkard! Did you ever see a nightbird, owl or screechowl, in the full sunlight, surrounded, hooted at by fledglings all around? When I had the opportunity much later, in my little garden at Cuverville, of being present one time at such a prodigious spectacle, I again thought immediately of that flock of scamps babbling around Verlaine; for it was he. His high hat had rolled to the ground, or more exactly into a puddle on the sidewalk, and that was what filled the brats with the most joy, for the stove-pipe, not usually worn in the morning except for special occasions, seemed the symbol of dignity itself. And Verlaine picked himself up, or rather picked himself up again, unkempt, haggard, his clothing in disorder and soiled with mud (he must have fallen down himself), holding up with one hand, I recall, his trousers without either belt or suspenders. . . . He looked like a wild boar or a deer, surrounded, worried by a pack of curs. And sometimes, as though answering the jeers with a blow from his snout, he bent toward the children angrily, crying, "Merde."[1]

More than half a century has passed. Paul Verlaine entered into glory a long time ago. I think those children, who were little more than ten years of age at that time (there were about twenty of them) . . . I think, perhaps, one of them will read this, and will say to himself: "If I had only known. . . ."

---

[1] A vulgar word, not translatable into decent English. Translator's note.

22

LITERARY MEMORIES AND PRESENT-DAY PROBLEMS[1]

"LITERARY MEMORIES?" "Present-day problems?" I hesitated between those two subjects, which at first seemed very different. Then, on reflecting over them, I understood that those two subjects interpenetrate and become one: for, in the often tragic light of recent events, the past becomes clear, and it is on looking for a present-day lesson in it, that I shall first bring out some memories.

As early as eighteen years of age, a young man makes up his mind to write. In school he is told and makes himself believe that to write well is first a matter of feeling and thinking correctly. He has read in the *Characters* of La Bruyère: "To make a book is a trade," otherwise expressed: something which can and must be learned.

As for painters, they serve an apprenticeship in the studio of some celebrated master; but as for the young man of letters, where can he go?

Pierre Louys and I were schoolmates; we had dis-

[1] Lecture given in Bayrouth in April and in Brussels in June 1946.

covered in each other with great delight if not exactly the same tastes, at least a commensurate love of poetry. Louys was more enterprising than I, bolder—but how gladly I allowed myself to be led by him.

He took me to Mallarmé's.

Mallarmé entertained every Tuesday evening in his little apartment on the rue de Rome. It has often been told, and very well, what those reunions were, and I should hesitate to speak to you of them again, if it were not to bring out certain traits of the poet's face, to clear up certain specific points in his teaching, that seem to me, from a distance, all the more remarkable because they were different from everything seen at that time, everything seen or said, or done to-day.

Nothing more modest than Mallarmé's home or his personal appearance. His salary as a teacher of English in the Lycée Condorcet did not permit him any luxury; but everything in his home was in excellent taste. The little dining-room where he entertained us could hold only eight persons, ten at the most, who sat around a table, where an enormous tobacco-jar had replaced the meal. The master himself remained standing, leaning against the brown faience stove. Madame Mallarmé had retired. Her daughter, Geneviève, at the stroke of ten, with smiling graciousness, brought in the toddies, sometimes waited a few minutes when there was not much company; but was too reserved to take part in the conversation. Mallarmé was almost the only one who talked. The *Divagations* which he published later give some fairly exact reflections of his remarks. But the tone of his voice, his smile, not on his lips but in his eyes, a circumspect smile, veiled, almost apprehensive, accompanied ordinarily by a furtive gesture: an index finger raised in sign of interrogation or expectation. . . . Oh, how far away we were, in that little room, on the rue de Rome, far from the vain noises of the busy city, from political reports, from corruption and intrigue. With Mallarmé we entered into a supra-sensible region, where money, honors and plaudits no longer counted; and nothing was more discreet, more secret than the radiance of his reputation. The whole cultivated world knows to-day—but, at that time, we were only a few exceptions who recognized it—that Mallarmé knew how to bring our classic poetry up to a degree of sonorous perfection, of plastic and inner beauty, of enchanting power never attained before, and that I believe it will never attain again—for, in art, what is perfect can not be come back to; one must go on, search elsewhere.

But there was something else in Mallarmé, and what shone from his personality was a sort of sanctity. In his domain, which was not of this world, he exercised a sort of priesthood. His remarks alone were addressed to our minds; his example touched our souls—oh! very simply, for he was not at all pontifical. Besides what he taught us by his example, as much and more than by his remarks (and that is what makes his face so important in my eyes), he taught us virtue. Yes, indeed, he appeared to me like a saint and as such I consider him; and I should like, in a brief panegyric, to lay stress on certain merits, extra-literary in appearance, but upon which literature, and our culture depend. The elements, the components, of that virtue? . . . A certain belief and confidence in truths absolute, intangible and unchangeable by circumstances, by events, by everything that, around Mallarmé, we used to call "contingencies." An attachment to a supra-sensible truth, before which everything gave way, faded out, became of little importance.

Oh! I see well, I see only too well where that contempt could lead: it invited you to turn your back on life. The poet lost contact with reality; he risked precipitating literature into abstract and glacial regions. May I be permitted to clarify this disdain of the outer world by an anecdote, for I should not like the example of Mallarmé to make my lecture too austere.

As a reaction against the Naturalist School and anxious to give Symbolism a novel it seemed to me to lack (for until then it had produced only poems), I had just written a certain *Voyage d'Urien*[1], of which the third and last part had appeared separately in booklet form in a separate reprint, under the misleading title *Voyage to Spitzberg*. I had sent this booklet to Mallarmé, who had received it with a slight raising of the eyebrows, thinking, from the title, that it was the story of a real periplus. On seeing me again a few days later: "Ah! you gave me a terrible fright; I was afraid you had gone there!" he said to me. And nothing was more exquisite than his smile.

A little later, it seemed to me necessary to establish a direct and sensuous contact between literature and the outer world and, as I wrote in a later preface to my *Nourritures Terrestres*[2], to "put a bare foot down on the ground again." On doing that, I made a departure from Mallarmé, to be sure, but I retained from his teaching a holy horror of easiness, of complacency, of everything that flatters and charms, both in literature and in life; an uncompromising love and need of sincerity, integrity, toward oneself and toward one's fellow-men; of the exigency, the unshakable conviction that, no matter what happens, what constitutes the value of man, his honor and his

---

[1] d'Urien, a pun on the words *du rien, all about nothing.* Translator's note.

[2] Just translated by Dorothy Bussy and published under the title *Fruits of the Earth.* Translator's note.

dignity, is more important, should be more important than all the rest and deserves that all the rest be subordinated to it, and, if need be, sacrificed.

One thing that seems to me worthy of notice and that I do not think has ever been remarked, at any rate sufficiently: an indirect consequence of that restlessness, of that integral love of what is true which is indistinguishable from the need for justice: it was in Mallarmé's immediate circle that, at the time of the celebrated Dreyfus affair, uncompromising justice recruited certain of its most ardent defenders—Ferdinand Hérold, Pierre Quillard, Bernard Lazare. . . . I was right then in saying that the teaching of the rue de Rome was not directed at the mind only, but strained at the formation of our souls. In that regard I should like to speak now of opportunism, and all the more willingly as to-day it is very much in style, under the form of *recruited literature.*

In Mallarmé's time, "recruited literature" had one illustrious representative, Maurice Barrès.

I am grateful to him for having been the first to notice my first book: *Les Cahiers d'André Walter.* This book, never having left the bookstore, was still piled up at Perrin's, Barrès' editor, where Barrès noticed it, and glanced at it. . . . The little of it that he read gave him the desire to know me. He communicated with me. At that time, I was hardly more than twenty years of age. Barrès was my elder by eight years. He already enjoyed considerable prestige among the young although he had not yet published more than a few volumes—those that form the consecrated series which he called *Le Culte du Moi.*[1] Besides he had directed all by himself a little magazine: *Taches d'encre,* of which he was the sole editor—that had only three numbers, but in which could be read a study of Baudelaire, which was not, which is not yet, well known, and that I consider one of the most remarkable, truly masterly! Masterly, Barrès was everywhere and ceaselessly, in his gestures, in his bearing, in the tone, haughty, ironical and scornful, of his voice. He imposed himself, as I suppose Chateaubriand must have done, whom to be sure he resembled closely. But larger of stature, better built, and breathing from his whole being a sort of authority somewhat scornful or condescending by which, nevertheless, one liked to be *taken in.* He charmed, but one approached him only in trembling. Very careful of his person, and always admirably dressed, with great elegance and a sort of genteel disorderliness at the same time. I recall his tall stature, his look a little equine (but that of a timid horse, if not a frightened one),—let us remember that Homer spoke of the bovine expression of Juno,—a very prominent, aquiline nose, very black

[1] *Egoism.* Translator's note.

locks of hair that he brought forward or allowed to fall over his fine forehead. . . . He might have been Spanish. Who was it said: We all resemble our bust (it was Richepin, I think)? Barrès, in love with Toledo, resembled a portrait of El Greco.

When a note from him invited me to pass a few minutes with him, my heart beat very hard. Harder yet, when I knocked on his door. He was then occupying what he calls "a certain little house in the Monceau section," one of the most elegant quarters in Paris. I have no exact remembrance of the conversation I had with him on that day. I was not precisely at my ease and Barrès helped little in bringing out and showing up personalities different from his own. I only remember this accurately: having to wait in a sort of lobby until the master was ready to receive me, I was admiring rows of very prettily bound books on the shelves of a kind of bookcase in that little room. Now Barrès had the reputation of reading little and boasted of it.

I had before me the complete works of Byron, and I committed the indiscretion of taking down one of the volumes. The whole series tumbled in one fell swoop. The books were dummies; it was a hidden compartment, the specious covering of a drawer, which contained (I closed it quickly) brushes and bottles of scent.

At that time Barrès exercised over a number of

young people an extraordinary prestige. The admiration that some of them offered him was a sort of devotion, worship. My friend, Maurice Quillot, to whom I later dictated my *Nourritures terrestres,* had a sort of niche constructed in his humble student's room where, instead of an icon, a large photograph of Barrès' portrait by Jacques-Emile Blanche received the homage of little lighted candles.

And I remember that same Maurice Quillot (ah! how young we were then!) invited me to share the expenses of a mass that we had said, at Saint-Séverin, for the repose of Barrès' soul—he had just married, not died.

Yes, Barrès read little. Scarcely more than Pierre Loti. If he was, nevertheless, very well informed, it was because his secretaries and friends read for him, furnished him arguments and adequate quotations.

Anything that could advance him more in his own direction, anchor his opinions, was what that great egotist looked for in books, in landscapes, in the spectacle of life. Unbelievably lacking in curiosity about others, I don't know whether he discovered or even simply recognized the value of any one of his contemporaries who was later to equal him in reputation, or lent the slightest attention to Jules Renard, to Proust, any more than to Claudel, Valéry or Giraudoux.

My relations with Barrès did not last long. After

the publication of the *Déracinés* (in 1897), I began to understand, to feel, or to foresee how harmful and even evil the theories he was emphasizing and that lured him along could be for healthy humanism and for us French. I am going to try to be specific about that.

Those theories, French or too exclusively French, those local truths specifically Lorrainese, Barrès opposed to Kant's doctrine, to what he called: "unhealthy Kantism." Why unhealthy? Because Kant founded his morality on general principles; because he had said: "Always act in such a way that you are willing for the maxim of your actions to be set up as a universal law." Now, according to Barrès, there could not be, in morality, any universal, any absolute; but only particular, opportune truths depending on happenings and places. The true, the good, were relative things, and each one of us should understand it, on listening to the lesson, the statement in *the land and the dead.*

Under a new aspect, it was the renewal of the old quarrel against the Jansenists. It was the "politics first" of Maurras and the *Action française.* It was already in germ, in force, the apology for the "false patriotism" of Colonel Henry, at the time of the Dreyfus affair, that is to say, without regard for the truth, the production of an apocryphal document, considered as opportune and serviceable, according to the famous saying: "The end justifies the means." Oh! that doctrine may well appear marvelous and of great assistance as long as you are the only one to make use of it. It is very nice, very practical, to teach the young Philippe Barrès, in *Les Amitiés françaises,* that the Germans have no souls, and that, therefore, with them, one can "go the limit." But who will prevent the Germans from soon reasoning in the same way, and this time at our expense? And you will see the fine theories of Barrès, when adopted by a neighboring enemy people, boomerang against us to slaughter us with their backfire. I recognize Barrès' lesson in Hitler.

But holding tight to his theories will be all important to Barrès, even more than the feeling of defeat and bankruptcy to which his theories lead us. We shall read in *Les Amitiés* (and I do not refrain from quoting to you a passage as significant, as deplorable, in which it is all mixed up together: the theory, the resolution, and some facile and false poetry or other . . .:

"No disaster (it was a question of the one of 1870), no disaster could deprive our sons of the enjoyment of knowing their submission to implacable laws, to necessity. Our sons will be well paid if they sometimes feel how it intoxicates the heart to overflowing, at the beginning of a glorious day, or under a steady rain, to carry a flower to a tomb, and to put into that act, whole armfuls, all our gardens, all our harvest of dreams." (p. 40).

Tombs, tombs, everywhere and always. To carry armloads of flowers to the tombs . . . in truth, that's what it is all about!

From the beginning, from the publication of the *Déracinés,* I rose up against Barrès, or at least against his doctrines. . . . From then on, I never ceased to revolt against him; to the degree that Massis, in his *Jugements,* could argue that my struggle against Barrès was my only reason for writing and that, without Barrès, I should not exist (a literary sense is understood). That, in spite of Massis, I was right to rise against Barrès, events, alas! have proved only too well. How blind were certain ones not to have understood at once, to have been so long in understanding where that would lead, sooner or later, necessarily. Moreover the *Action française* has survived, and I think that the French youth of to-day no longer read Barrès (they are wrong), in any case they no longer follow him (they do well). A curious and significant thing: to-day it is in the camp of the adversary, it is among the communists, that the ravages of the relativist doctrines are now making themselves felt, that of "the end justifies the means." I think them marvelously well-fitted to pervert judgment, sometimes forever. They are the cause of the worst errors, in private life as in politics, and I do not think that one can, with impunity, ever compromise with the truth—let us say, if you prefer: God.

No more than Maurras was Barrès a believer. Religion, for him, inherited from *The Land and the Dead,* is an integral part of his opportunism; it touched his heart sentimentally, but offered his mind nothing absolute. He sets down in his book *Les Amitiés françaises* (that Thibaudet, formed by him, considered one of his best)—he sets down, I said, the principles of the education he gives to his son. What appears most important to him, is to inculcate in the child Philippe the feeling of attachment, of attachment "to the land and our dead." That is what seems to him "fundamental." "It is fitting," he writes, "it is sweet that the same inner music should regulate the steps of those who set out on the path to our tombs, and those who have already gone half the way." He tries to give to his son "the knowledge of our predestination" and would consider himself fortunate if it could be said later, quoting a line of Heredia:

In spite of himself, he made the hereditary gesture,

excluding all spontaneity, as he again says: "substituting for his instinctive tendency a determined pattern."

The almost unconscious struggle against this instinct sometimes leads the work of Barrès into a most disturbing complexity; but it is the pages on which this "instinctive tendency" gives itself the freest rein that retain the greatest chance of survival and that can still touch us: the passages on Venice or Toledo, on the Orontes and, in the compact mass of the *Déracinés,* the refreshing tale of Astiné Aravian; each time, as a matter of fact that our Lorrainese abandons himself, lets himself go without fear of his inconsistencies, forgetting to be what he wants to be, consenting to show himself in his natural state: a man and no longer only a Lorrainese.

For—and the remark has often been made—the greatness, the value, the benefit of our French culture is that it is not, if I may say so, of local interest. The methods of thought, the truths it teaches us, are not particularly Lorrainese and consequently do not risk backfiring against us when adopted by a neighboring people. They are general, human, susceptible of touching the most diverse peoples; and since, in them, every human being can learn to know himself, can recognize and communicate with himself, they work not toward division and opposition, but toward conciliation and understanding.

I hasten to add this, as it appears to me of primordial importance: French literature, taken as a whole, does not tend in one direction alone . . . (I am thinking of the exquisite remark of Madame de

Sévigné, who said of herself: "I am far from being of my own opinion," thus indicating that she retained over herself and the natural bent of her sensibility, a critical judgment without complacency.) French thought at every period of its development, of its history, presents to our attention a dialogue, a pathetic and unending dialogue, a dialogue worthy as any to occupy (for on listening to it, one takes part in it) both our minds and our hearts—and I consider that a young mind concerned about our culture and eager to let itself be instructed by it, I consider that that mind would be deflected, if it heeded, or if it were allowed to hear, only one of the two voices of the dialogue—a dialogue not at all between a political right and left, but, much deeper and more vital, between secular tradition, the submission to recognized authority, and free thinking, the spirit of doubt, self-examination that works toward a slow and progressive emancipation of the individual. We already see it outlined in the struggle between Abélard and the Church,—the latter, needless to say, always triumphs, but on withdrawing and reforming its positions each time on this side of its first lines. The dialogue is taken up again with Pascal against Montaigne. There is no exchange of remarks between them, since Montaigne is dead when Pascal begins to speak; yet it is to him he addresses himself—and not only in the illustrious conversation with Monsieur de Sacy. It is to Montaigne's *Essays* that the book of *Pensées*[1] is opposed, and on which, it could be said, he bases everything. "The foolish idea he had of depicting himself," he said of Montaigne, without foreseeing that the passages in the *Pensées* where Pascal too depicts himself and lets himself go, with his anguish and his doubt, touch us to-day more than the statement of his dogmatics. In the same way, what we admire in Bossuet is not the antiquated theologian, it is the perfect art of his admirable language, which makes him one of the magnificent writers of our literature: without that art he would scarcely be read to-day. It is due to that form, which he himself considered impious, that he survives.

Dialogue recommenced ceaselessly across the ages and more or less dissembled on the side of free-thinking, by wisdom, that "wisdom of the serpent," as the Holy Scriptures say, for the tempting and liberating demon of the mind prefers to speak in a whisper; he insinuates, while the believer proclaims, —and Descartes takes as his motto *larvatus prodeo,* "I advance with a mask on,"—or better said, it is under a mask that I advance.

And sometimes one of the voices wins: in the eighteenth century, it was that of free-thinking, masked no longer. It won to the point of bringing

---

1 *Thoughts.* Translator's note.

about, as a necessary result, a distressing drying up of poetic enthusiasm. But the balance of the dialogue is never disturbed for long, in France. With Chateaubriand and Lamartine, the religious sentiment, a source of lyricism, wells up magnificently. It is the great Romantic flood. And, if Michelet and Hugo revolt against the Church and the churches, it is still with a profound religious feeling.

Rolling from one bank to the other, the vessel of French culture progresses and pursues its hazardous route, *fluctuat nec mergitur*—it sails on and will never be sunk. It would risk being so, it would be, on the day one of the two interlocutors of the dialogue should be definitely victorious over the other and reduce him to silence, on the day when the ship should upset or roll over on one side.

In our day, we watch a prodigious unfolding of Catholic writers: after Huysmans and Léon Bloy, Jammes, Péguy, Claudel, Mauriac, Gabriel Marcel, Bernanos, Maritain . . . but without speaking of a Proust or a Suarès, the solid and unwavering Paul Valéry would suffice to balance them. Never was the spirit of criticism exercised in a more masterly way on the most diverse problems, and never had it been able to prove itself more creative. Now I recall Oscar Wilde's remark: "Imagination imitates; it is the spirit of criticism that creates," a remark that Baudelaire could have made and that it would profit every artist to meditate upon. (It is not a question, needless to say, of criticizing others, but oneself.) For among the multitudinous phantasms that the imagination offers us in disorderly fashion, the critical mind must choose—every design implies a choice—and it is a school of design that I admire especially in France.

When, with a few rare friends about me, we founded the *Nouvelle Revue Française,* which, later, was to assume an unhoped for importance, people at first were determined to see in it the formation of a little "clique" and, as happens all too often: a "mutual admiration society." Now it was exactly the contrary: "a Society of Criticism," it could have been called—and of mutual criticism. That satisfaction with oneself toward which, when one is young and a man of letters, one is generally only too easily inclined, we feared to the degree that we had promised, from the very beginning, never to speak of each other in the magazine. But not a reader noticed that discretion; for silences are little remarked—and yet they are often very significant and important.

Another specialty (if I may say so) of the *Nouvelle Revue Française,* and it was certainly noticed but very little understood, was to judge the writings it published only on their merit and not at all on their tendencies, to accept the excellent without regard to its color,—which allowed it to offer the best.

And so, under the cover of the *Nouvelle Revue Française* was continued the dialogue of which I was speaking just now, with constant concern on our part to maintain the equilibrium of the thought, by means of weights.

That does not look like anything but it is enormous, and I believe that our magazine was the only one not to show itself, in one direction or the other, tendentious. That is what aroused the periodic indignation of Claudel, who protested furiously when he saw, alongside of one of his articles, even if it were at the beginning of a number, an article by Proust, Suarès, Valéry or de Léautaud that seemed to challenge him. It was to this wise eclecticism that the *Nouvelle Revue Française* owed its extraordinary progressive success, in foreign countries as well as in France; for I do not know a single author of real merit, often unknown at first, who was not launched or sheltered by us.

Of course, I am only speaking of the pre-war *Nouvelle Revue Française*—before the attitude of a new imposed directorship had forced, alas! the best of its former collaborators to withdraw.

By the juxtaposition of the articles offered, the *Nouvelle Revue Française* was again and above all a school of thought. It excelled in criticism and contributed greatly to sweeping the literary sky clean of false values, in restoring the cult of the great and healthy tradition, of style and the pure design of thought. It is apparent to-day, I believe, that it did a great deal toward "defending" and "rendering illustrious" our culture. And I lack time to speak of what could be considered as its off-shoot: the theatre of the *Vieux Colombier.*

Then the war came. A huge war, apocalyptic, which imperilled and endangered everything that was closest to our hearts: the very dignity of man and whatever it is that gives us our reason for living.

It is necessary to take all that up again, to begin again on new foundations. I say: on new foundations —for I am convinced we can not find salvation in a simple return and attachment to the past. Everything must be questioned.

To be sure we have watched a remarkable and almost miraculous rebirth of France. A courageous youth has covered itself with glory, has deserved the gratitude of its elders. And this fact is all the more admirable because war, for its sacrifices, chooses the best who are the first to devote themselves, to offer themselves. It operates a sort of inverse selection and skims off the elite of the country. But the peculiar combative virtues that permitted the rebirth of France are not the same ones that are necessary for the reestablishment of order, once peace is reconquered and assured. Montesquieu considers that what constitutes the extraordinary vitality of France is the diversity of its genius. Yesterday, hardy combatants were needed, to-day it is architects, and there will be some. The need we have of them will bring them to life, and they will respond to the call.

I have great hope; but it must be recognized that our youth, following that frightful upheaval, remains deeply shaken. Under a woefully starless sky, the youth of to-day—at least that new Existentialist school that makes so much noise to-day, that important part of youth, seems to take as its own the gloomy affirmation which I read in the same book of Barrès' I was quoting:

"From whatever point one considers it, the universe and our existence are senseless confusion."

And more recently we heard Roger Martin du Gard (or at least one of his heroes) and Jean Rostand repeat—after Barrès, but before Camus, Sartre and the Existentialists of to-day: "We live in an absurd world where nothing rimes with anything. . . ."

Well! I should like to say to the young people disoriented by the absence of faith: to make the world rime with something is up to you alone!

It is up to man, and man is the starting point. The world, this absurd world, will stop being absurd; it is up to you alone. The world will be what you make it.

The more you tell me and insist there is nothing absolute in this world and in our sky, that truth, justice and beauty are man's creations, the more I insist that it is then up to man to maintain them, that his honor demands it. Man is responsible to God.

There is not a country, however protected it may have been, however far from the field of battle, that has not been more or less reached by the shadow of the new problems, no people that does not feel itself a little liable, no thinking youth who does not ask himself disturbing and serious questions.

I shall not look for any other proof than the letter I received a little before leaving Egypt. That letter from a young student in Bagdad seemed to me so typical and so eloquent that I want to read you the principal paragraphs in it.

"Pardon a stranger for writing you. I believe the writer is responsible for what he writes.

"You have habituated us, in your books, to a certain perpetual and invigorating restlessness. That restlessness you have taught us is the only hope of a generation sacrificed in advance."

Those words wrung my heart. I had often heard them; in France and elsewhere, numerous young people consider themselves a part of a "sacrificed generation." . . . Useless to tell you that I protest with all my heart against that idea.

I continue the reading of the letter:

"I shall say more; that restlessness is our only

nobility. In a word, the gist of your teaching is that we should accept nothing, or consider anything acquired in advance. Now, in the letter my friend X. received from you, I was surprised and disappointed, I confess, to see that you exhort him to hope, because "without hope," you said, "souls faint and become feeble."

Here I open the parenthesis. I did not know the young man to whom I was writing that letter at all. He had written an article in Arabic about me, an article that I couldn't read, and, as I nevertheless felt the desire to express my sympathy to him, I could do it only in a very indefinite way, so I employed vague terms and, I recognize, unfortunately trite.

So I continue my reading:

"To accept hope, Master, is not what you can propose to us now. In these times of suffering and distress, which have just begun, to accept hope would be to fall down, for, even if we are to see better days in our lifetime, it is surely not by contenting ourselves with hoping that we shall find them.

"No, we must not hope, but remain perpetually restless. That is the only attitude I believe worthwhile and which can safeguard our *integrity*.

"So tell me, Master, what you think of it, and whether you believe I am right. Everything of yours that I have read leads me to suppose so, and that is why that sentence in your letter to my friend frightened me. It seems to me that it invites to an abdication of what appears to me our last pretension to nobility.

"Tell me if it is so."

How could I answer such a fine letter, and one that moved me all the more because it came from a country that I had thought far away and little touched by the happenings, not very much exposed to our culture?

Oh! my answer is very simple.

At a time when I feel in such great peril, so besieged on all sides, that which constitutes the value of man, his honor and his dignity, all that we live for, our reason for living—it is just knowing that among the young people, there are some, even though they be very small in number, and from any country whatever—who do not rest, who maintain intact their moral and intellectual *integrity,* and protest against every word of a totalitarian nature and every enterprise that claims to bend, subordinate, subject thought, diminish the soul—for in the last analysis it is the soul that is in question—it is knowing that they are there, those young men, that they are living, they, the salt of the earth; that is just what sustains us, their elders; that is what permits me, already as old and ready to leave life as I am, not to die in despair.

I believe in the virtue of the common people. I believe in the virtue of the small number.

The world will be saved by a few.

23

PREFACE TO VOL DE NUIT[1]

FOR the airplane companies, it was a question of vying in speed with the other means of transportation. That is what Rivière, the admirable figure of a captain in this book, will explain: "For us it is a question of life or death, since each night we lose the advantage gained over the railroads and the ships during the day. This nightly service, much criticized at first, then accepted, and become practical after the risk of the first experiments, was still, at the time of this story, very dangerous; to the impalpable perils of the aerial routes strewn with surprises, can now be added the treacherous mystery of the night. However great the risks still are, I hasten to say that they become less and less each day, each new trip facilitating the next one and making it a little safer. But just as there is a first heroic period for the exploration of unknown lands, so there is for aviation, and *Vol de Nuit,* which depicts for us the tragic adventure of one of those pioneers of the air, naturally takes on an epic tone.

[1] *Night-Flight.* Translator's note.

I like Saint-Exupéry's first book, but this one even more. In *Courrier-Sud*[2] a sentimental intrigue, which brings the hero close to us, is mingled with the memories of the aviator and noted with striking exactitude. Ah! how human we feel him to be, how vulnerable, in his susceptibility to tenderness. The hero of *Vol de Nuit,* not dehumanized to be sure, rises to superhuman courage. I think that what especially pleases me in this thrilling story, is its nobility. The weaknesses, the abandons, the downfalls of man, we know only too well, and the literature of our times is only too skillful in denouncing them; but this transcendence of oneself, obtained only by a straining of the will, is what we need above all to have someone demonstrate to us.

Still more astonishing than the character of the aviator appears to me that of Rivière, his captain. He does not act himself; he makes others act, breathes courage into his pilots, demands from them their best, and constrains them to valor. His relentless determination does not tolerate weakness, and, by him, the slightest flinching is punished. At first glance, his severity appears inhuman, excessive. But it is to the imperfections that it is applied, not to the man himself, that Rivière intends to form. Throughout this picture can be felt the admiration of the author. I am particularly grateful to him for throw-

[2] *Southern Mail.* Translator's note.

ing light on this paradoxical truth that, for me, is of considerable psychological importance: that the happiness of man is not in liberty, but in the acceptance of a duty. Everyone of the characters in this book is ardently, totally devoted to what he *ought* to do, to that dangerous task in whose accomplishment alone he will find the repose of happiness. And one perceives that Rivière is by no means callous (nothing more touching than the story of the visit he received from the wife of the lost pilot) and that it requires no less courage for him to give orders than for his pilots to execute them.

"To make oneself loved," he will say, "pity is sufficient. I do not pity very much, or I conceal it. . . . I am surprised at my power sometimes." And again: "Love those whom you command, but without telling them so."

Thus it is that the sentiment of duty dominates Rivière; "the hidden sentiment of duty, greater than that of loving." Let not man's aim be himself, but subordination and sacrifice to something which dominates him and lives on him. And I like to find here again that "hidden sentiment" that made my Prometheus say, paradoxically: "I do not love man, I love what devours him." That is the source of all heroism: "We act," thought Rivière, "as though something surpassed human life in value. . . . But what?" And again: "Perhaps something else to save, something more durable, exists; perhaps it is to save that part of man that Rivière works." We do not doubt it.

At a time when the idea of heroism tends to desert the army, since the manly virtues risk remaining without employment in to-morrow's wars of which the chemists invite us to foresee the future horror, is it not in aviation that we see courage displayed most admirably and usefully? The pilot, who risks his life continuously, has some right to smile at the idea that we generally have of "courage." Will Saint-Exupéry permit me to quote one of his letters, already old; it goes back to the time when he was flying over the Mauritania to ensure the service between Casablanca and Dakar:

"I do not know when I shall return, I have so much work to do: searching for lost comrades; repair service for planes fallen in disaffected territories, and some mail services for Dakar.

"I have just succeeded in a little exploit: passed two days and two nights with eleven Moors and a mechanic to save a plane. Various and serious alerts. For the first time, I have heard bullets whistling over my head. At last I know what I am in this atmosphere: much calmer than the Moors. But I have come to understand too, something that had always surprised me: why Plato (or Aristotle?) puts courage in the last line of virtues. It is not made up of very fine feelings: a little anger, a little vanity, a great deal of obstinacy and an ordinary sporting pleasure. Above all the excitement of physical strength which, nevertheless, has nothing to do with it. You cross your arms over your open shirt and take a deep breath. It is rather agreeable. When that takes place at night, there is mixed with it the feeling of having committed a great stupidity. Never again will I admire a man who is merely courageous."

I could add, as an epigraph to that quotation, an apothegm taken from the book of Quinto (that I am far from approving always):

"One conceals one's bravery like one's love"; or better said: "The brave hide their acts as upright people their charity. They disguise them or make excuses for them."

Everything that Saint-Exupéry relates, he speaks of "in full knowledge of the facts." The personal facing of frequent danger gives his book an authentic and inimitable flavor. We have had numerous war stories or imaginary adventures in which the author sometimes gives evidence of versatile talent, but which makes real adventurers or combatants who read it smile. This tale, whose literary merit I admire also, has, besides, documentary value, and these two qualities, so unexpectedly united, give to *Vol de Nuit* its exceptional importance.

24

PREFACE TO SOME RECENT WRITINGS BY THOMAS MANN[1]

I HOLD it a great honor to preface this little book. Thomas Mann is one of the rare men to-day whom we can admire without reserve. In his work there is not one failure, and there is not one in his life. His retort to an absurd Hitlerian insult is worthy of the author of *Buddenbrock*, of the *Magic Mountain* and of the *Joseph* trilogy. The importance of the work gives its importance and its powerful significance to the gesture.

Henceforth Thomas Mann is Czechoslovakian. Recently I saw him again at Kusnacht, in the vicinity of Zurich, where he had taken exile. I recognized with deep feeling that gentleness of manners and that delicate charm which conceal a great firmness of character and an inflexible determination. The same that I admire in his wife too, and that can

[1] Collected in the volume *Avertissement à l'Europe* (*Warning to Europe*), translated from the German by Rainer Riemel (Gallimard, end of 1937).

be encountered again in his children with, sometimes, a charming boisterousness.

For Thomas Mann was not banished; the Germans in Germany insist on that point.

"Nothing," say they, "forced him to leave a country from which no particular proscription drove him. It was up to him alone to remain, just as we are doing, and to recognize with us that one can very well accommodate himself to a regime that asks us, after all, only to acquiesce. He was "pig-headed." So much the worse for him. Everything else came as a result of it; both the confiscation of his property in Bavaria; and the final withdrawal of his German citizenship and his title at the University of Bonn."

Thomas Mann took no part in public affairs. "I was born to bear witness in serenity rather than in martyrdom, to bring a message of peace to the world rather than to nourish conflict and hatred," he tells us in the beautiful letter to be read. Doubtless; but he was "born to bear witness"; that is his role; that of a man of letters; and when a despotic government projects the subordination of the mind, not to let one's mind be twisted is taking part in politics. What Sainte-Beuve said of the "politics" of André Chénier could be applied to him: "It is not a concerted and sustained action; it is an individual protestation, logical in its persistency, lyrical in its source and flow, the protestation of an upright man who braves those whom he refutes at the same time that he does not fear to provoke the sword against himself." Fortunately it is no longer a question of the guillotine in this case; but Thomas Mann is absolutely correct in writing: "If I had remained in Germany, or if I had returned to it, I should probably be no longer living." Thomas Mann was contrained by his very honesty to assume a political role, in a country where "honest people" who still meddle with thinking become nuisances and sedition-mongers. As for us, we have enough love for Germany to recognize her voice much better in Thomas Mann's protestations than in the letter of the Dean of the University of Bonn. In that protestation, indignation is still restrained; Thomas Mann will let it appear more where Spain is concerned, in the third of the writings that are collected here. And I see with admiration that this indignation shows itself more lively where personal interest is less involved. That is how we can recognize the perfect sincerity of those pages; not only are they from the same man, but from the same ink, the same inspiration; an equal conviction animates them. No, it is not personal interest that dictates them; Mann remains genuinely on the spiritual side; a *humanist,* in the fullest sense of the word.

Humanism—he explains to us in a discourse pronounced at Budapest on the occasion of debates organized recently by the Institute of Intellectual Cooperation—"Humanism . . . is scholarly in nothing and has, directly, nothing to do with erudition. Humanism is rather a *spirit,* an intellectual disposition, a state of the human mind that implies justice, liberty, knowledge and tolerance, amenity and serenity; doubt also, not as an end in itself, but as a search for the truth, an effort filled with concern to free this truth from the presumptions of those who put that truth under a bushel." He said first: "Would not the best and simplest be to look on humanism as *the contrary of fanaticism?*"

Humanism, such as Thomas Mann presents it here, may seem, in these calm periods, related to a sort of pleasing Renanism; but don't be deceived; let the time come when force will try to bend the mind, to submit it to some arbitrary and brutal regulation, immediately the genuine humanist takes consciousness of his role; refusing to bow, he opposes to material force another force: that indomitable force of the mind whose signal merit every tyrant, whether he will or no, has to recognize.

If I have insisted on quoting the sentences just read, it is because the discourse from which they are extracts does not figure in this volume. But all the pages that can be read further on render the same true, full sound. Certain truths that are set forth there should invite young people to reflect; in particular this one: "The youth (of to-day) do not know culture in its most elevated and deepest sense. They know nothing of the work on oneself. They no longer know anything about individual responsibility, and find all their comforts in collective life. *Collective life, compared to individual life, is the sphere of ease.* Ease which goes to the worst of relinquishments. This generation wants only to say farewell forever to its own personality. What it wants, what it loves, is intoxication. It will find its final end in a new war where our civilization will perish.

The flood of barbarism that Thomas Mann anxiously sees unfurling over our old world has not yet reached France; and that is why, perhaps, I, a Frenchman, feel a little less cast down than he. But how can I help recognizing the justice of the reflections he develops in his *Warning to Europe?* "The highest values are no longer safe from destruction," he says, "and, perhaps, the destiny of our entire civilization." He refuses to hold the war of 1914 responsible for the present degradation. His *Buddenbrock,* by painting us through three generations, "the history of the decline of a family," gives witness to the torment that already dwelt in him in 1901. "I repeat," he writes, "today, that the failure of European culture is not the achievement of the war, which only hastened it and made it more apparent."

And very subtly, but very wisely too, he tries to demonstrate that, having arrived at a certain stage, culture reaches the point of taking up a position against itself. "In all humanism, there is an element of weakness," he remarks, "which comes from its repugnance for fanaticism, from its tolerance and its leaning toward indulgent scepticism; in a word: from its natural beauty. And that can, in certain circumstances, become fatal."

Without a doubt, the present Hitlerian regime puts culture in great danger; but Thomas Mann sees the worst danger in this that, in our times, reason is generally scoffed at, and the one who denies reason, in the name of Life, appears more intelligent than the reasonable being.

"Perhaps the world is lost already," he concludes. "It surely is if it does not succeed in tearing itself away from that hypnosis and becoming conscious of itself once more." That is the labor of the pages you have here. And, thanks to them, I may think: No, Thomas Mann; no; our world is not yet lost; it can not be so as long as a voice like yours is still raised to warn it. As long as consciences like yours remain awake and faithful, we shall not despair.

25

PREFACE
FOR A FRENCH TRANSLATION BY JEAN LAMBERT OF MORGENLANDFAHRT (A TRIP TO THE ORIENT) BY HERMANN HESSE

WHILE the world conference was taking place at Geneva, that I was afraid would be too tiring for me to take part in, I answered the appeal of young teachers and students of various nationalities gathered together in the vicinity of Innsbruck.

Nothing less solemn, more simply cordial than that assembly initiated by the French. I took the floor to repeat almost exactly what I had previously said in Alexandria, Beyrouth, then in Brussels: that our occidental culture appeared to me in grave danger; besieged on the right and the left by totalitarian doctrines into which all individuality had been reabsorbed.

"I believe in the virtue of a small number . . . The world will be saved by a few." It is on the confession of a like conviction, expressed in almost the same words that the last book of Hesse ends: *Frieden und Krieg*, of which the last chapter alone is recent. The large number of articles he groups together is inspired by the other war and its consequences. From the beginning of Hitlerism, he foresaw the dangers of that sinister adventure into which Germany, with blind-folded eyes, was about to let herself be led.

In Pertisau, during the course of a little unofficial congress, someone asked how it happened that not a voice in Germany was raised in time to denounce the danger, and, perhaps, by denouncing it, to prevent it. "He who remains silent, approves. Germany, unanimous in its error, should be unanimously condemned." I protested that that was to fail to recognize the many clandestine efforts and the heroic opposition of the churches, both Catholic and Protestant. One had to see in this general silence not so much indifference or submission, as muzzling. Totalitarianism, in this case as almost always, obtained only precarious results, and by what cruel means: censorship of writings, death, prison, exile, for those who would have liked to speak. May we in France never know a time when the dissenters would be reduced to silence in such a way! Merit is on the side of the small number; on the side of those who do not belong to a party, or, at least, who, even if they are enrolled (and that is then called "voluntary enlistment") keep their consciences clean, their minds free and speak openly. They are rare; but the importance of their voices can be recognized by that very dissonance. It is it, it is they, who will be listened to later.

During the entire Hitlerian period, Hesse's writings were banned in Germany. Even to-day printed in Switzerland, they have acquired, through repression, a power of expansion all the greater. Some of his books, translated into French, had appeared well before the war, but had remained little noticed. In our time, one scarcely pays heed to anything except explosives, and restrained writings hang fire. When they have real merit, it is rarely until several years after that their furrow spreads and widens.

With Hesse the expression alone is restrained, not the feeling or the thought; and what tempers the expression of these is the exquisite feeling of fitness, reserve and harmony, and, with relationship to cosmos, the interdependence of things; it is also a certain latent irony, of which few Germans seem to me capable, and whose total absence so often spoils so many works by so many of their authors, who take themselves terribly seriously. It is difficult to explain this, for we in France, to be sure, fall willingly into the opposite excess, and I am far from making the apology for our faults. For the narrow-minded convictions of Rousseau, I would often yield the most amusing maliciousness of Voltaire; but with Pascal, for instance, how much the laughter in the *Provinciales* deepens for me the gravity of the *Pensées*!

Schumann had this irony, with or without Heine, and I love the title he gives to one of his "Scenes of Children": "Fast zu ernst!"[1] What I have especially retained from *Wilhelm Tell* (apart from the springtide song that opens the play) is, at the beginning of Act 2, the first words of Walter Furst's wife, when she sees her husband all weighed down by cares that he has not yet related: "So ernst, mein Freund!" "So serious, my dear!" I shall have to reread that play. . . . Serious, does Schiller know how not to be so always?—and that is too much.

There are bitter ironies where bile and peccant humors pour out; but Hesse's, so charming in quality, seems to me to depend on the faculty of leaving himself behind, of seeing himself without looking, of judging himself without complacency[2]; it is a form of modesty that becomes all the more attractive because more gifts and virtues accompany it.

---

[1] "Almost too serious."

[2] Such also is the humor of which he speaks in his *Steppenwolf:* "You have to learn to laugh. To attain a higher form of humor, cease first to take yourself too seriously."

Hesse is a painter almost as much as a poet. In certain of his collections of verse, the reproduction of a watercolor accompanies the poem as an illustration; it is of an almost childlike docility; so natural and translating a communion with the outer world, so harmonious and so perfect that no disturbance of the soul can find an access to it. It is a work of art. However diverse (in subject matter if not in tendency) may be Hesse's books that I have read, I recognize in each of them the same pagan love of Nature: a sort of devotion. The open air circulates through their pages that quiver with panicky breaths, like the leaves of forest trees. In each of them, too, I refind the same indecision of soul; its contours are illusive and its aspirations, infinite; it is infatuated with vague sympathies, ready for the reception of any chance *imperative;* little determined by the past to find in submission itself an aim, a reason for living, an anchor for his floating impulses. Such, moreover, is the German soul of which Hesse, in spite of his resistance (which is explained by other and very rare virtues), remains one of the most representative witnesses. For something primitive lingers in the Germanic soul when not ameliorated by culture; a sort of functional availability; subject to the call of the seasons, of encounters and a proposed ideal to which to devote themselves without critical examination or haggling. From then on you understand easily what facile prey these souls will be, spontaneously disposed to abnegation. Indolently they allow themselves to be seized by a sort of voluptuousness brought about by non-resistance, the almost feminine abandon to the invitation of anything at all triumphant: enthusiasm, vague effusions, thirst for conquest and limitless expansion. . . . Let us add this too, as a corollary: a somewhat gregarious need to group themselves, to form *Bund,* a more or less secret society, and to wend their way in company toward an end often ill-defined, in appearance all the more noble because it is colored by mysticism and remains rather mysterious. That is, strictly speaking, the subject even of this book; and so it seems to me, in spite of its specious form, strangely revealing.

And everything that I say here would predispose Hesse to acceptance, would have offered him as a docile and easy victim to this totalitarian mirage that charms, even to-day, so many of the indecisive and so many "voluntary recruits"—had it not been for the singular virtue he advocates, that he declares he cherishes above all, that he considers superior to all other virtues, and which he deeply regrets that the German soul so often lacks lamentably; he calls it *Eigensinn,* a word that means at the same time confidence in oneself and consciousness of oneself. In a writing dated 1919 which he has just brought out again, he speaks of it excellently. All the human virtues (about the way he expresses it) are embodied in a single nomenclature alone: obedience. But it is a question of knowing to what. The *Eigensinn* itself is assimilated into obedience; but while all the other virtues, the most preached and the most beloved, go back or refer to laws that men have invented, this supreme virtue alone heeds and respects only *itself*. That this virtue isolates you goes without saying; and opposes you to the masses, and points you out to the fury of the chiefs and directors of the herd. Hesse paid with exile; and others with imprisonment and death.

Again he says in a short writing that all creatures under the sun live and develop as they wish and according to their own laws; man alone allows himself to be fashioned and bent by the laws that others have made. The entire work of Hesse is a poetic effort for emancipation with a view to escaping imitation and reassuming the genuineness compromised. Before teaching it to others, it is necessary to preserve it in oneself. Hesse arrives at it through culture. Although profoundly and fundamentally German, it is only by turning his back on Germany that he succeeds. Those in his country who were able to remain loyal to themselves, and not to allow themselves to be deflected are rare; it is to them he addresses himself and says: however few you may be, it is in you, and you alone, that the virtue of Germany has taken refuge and it is on you that her future depends.

With them we can come to an understanding. With them we should speak.

26

LETTER-PREFACE
TO THE POEMS OF JEAN LACAZE

Dear Sir,

HOW could I not yield to your appeal? But then you must permit me to quote, in the course of this preface, a few lines from your letter which explain and motivate it. For it concerns this grave question: the responsibility of the writer, and, in the present case, so painful and glorious, of my influence in particular which, you say, played such an important role in the formation of your son (am I to understand also: in his final decision?): . . . *"Your morality had become his! And how I had to fight you!"* In a word, you hold me responsible; but you add immediately: *"And now, I no longer know . . . I am not angry with you any more. On the contrary. . . ."*[1] Then, as a recognition of his feelings,

[1] The suspension points are not mine.

you inform me of your *"great desire to see* (my) *name near his in the publication of his poetic work."* And your letter ended with this sentence (of which a few words only call for a protest that I am going to express): *"Perhaps you will answer me favorably, or, rather, disregarding the father, and thinking of the sacrifice of the son, of the sacrifice of all the young men who died because their souls were too fine and had nothing to do among us, would you be willing, by honoring one of them, to honor them all?"* Yes, to be sure, and with all my heart; but first I protest: how can you say of that soul of your child so noble and fine, and of those who are like him, that "they have nothing to do among us?" Exactly the contrary, we greatly need their beauty, their nobility; and if their sacrifice has saved France, the sacrifice of the best, France remains lamentably impoverished by it. At any rate, that is not how the matter should be presented; you must think: Without doubt these griefs are frightful; so much promise, so much hope—but it is thanks to that signal holocaust that France can be born again to-day. It is to your son, it is to those who died as he died, that our gratitude and that of a reborn fatherland is extended.

My influence has been much spoken about. And not with approval. Some consider me a perverting influence. I had this inner satisfaction of seeing the young who claimed kinship with me (and every one of my real friends) enter into the Resistance one after the other, while my most noteworthy accusers of yesterday. . . . That was also because the latter represented submission to an established order, in whose very name they condemned me, however arbitrary that order might be; the others, revolt, liberty of thought, emancipation of the mind and exactingness toward themselves; and such is the principle teaching those young "disciples" had been able to extract from my writings. I retain for your son that particular gratitude for having proved, in an exemplary fashion, that they can nourish heroes. "Influence does not create; it awakens," I said back in 1900, in my first lecture—and I am satisfied if my books have been able to help young people to ascertain and liberate whatever of the heroic was sleeping in them. To raise man above himself, to deliver him from his weight, to help him go beyond himself, by exalting him, reassuring him, warning him, tempering him, is not that the secret aim of literature? Not, to be sure, the only one, but the highest, the best, and the one from which, in these recent times, it has turned aside most unfortunately. I say the *secret* aim, for nothing is worse than edifying, moralizing, stupefying. But if the artist, as he works, should concern himself only with the plastic qualities of his writings, the esthetics and morality, almost without his knowing it, are intermingled in it.

"Your Nourritures terrestres *were his breviary,"* you write me. *"How many times have I heard him repeat with rapture: ". . . Melancholy is only the lapsing of fervor." He loved life. . . . He said to you* (And you quote some lines by him, dedicated to me, to which his death has given an increase of tragic meaning):

Oh! I am afraid
And I don't want to die.
For life is precious and singular
And I have not lived enough . . .

You add: *"His life! . . . He had a talent for living it beautifully. He gave it. Knowing he was giving it."*

In the long poem he entitled "Departure Songs," he wrote with clairvoyant consciousness and a sort of foresight into his tragic destiny:

I am going to leave in the Pale Light of dawn
For a Death eternal and joyous
That will cleanse my heart
Of its grief and love
I shall never return
And that, perhaps, is better

* * * *

I must leave behind for all time
Familiar and weighty things—like chains
I must cast aside with a shrug of the shoulder

The Past—behind my back,
And see before me only a single, straight road
Opening before life—before Death.
O bitter despair of the inevitable
Parting!
—And never shall I return . . .

This poem dates from the beginning of July 1944; the 17th of August Jean Lacaze joined a group of the maquis. You copied for me the letter that you found on his table, after his clandestine departure. I am transcribing the first lines with deep emotion: "*My dear Parents,*

I am leaving. This decision that I have put off for a long time out of consideration for you, I must take to-day. The national uprising is near. General de Gaulle has ordered every unwounded man to join up with the maquis by whatever means possible. I consider that it would be shameful cowardice on my part to remain here at this time. And so I am going. . . ."

Three days after Jean Lacaze, with about twenty comrades, threw himself into the attack of a closed column of Germans. As bold as that sortie was in open territory, your only son alone was hit.

I do not know, Sir, what your son's career would have been. His first verses, by their ingenuity, permit us to hope. If I had known, I would have set my heart on aiding so many smiling promises with my confidence. . . .

What a great advantage faith would be here! It alone permits efficacious consolation, the assurance of a future life, with recognition and retribution. . . . I beg you to see a mark of esteem in my refusal to try to console you. You should, we should remain inconsolable. It is in our memory, in the memory of those who loved him, that your son survives—and in that incomplete work by which he has surrendered the purest and best part of himself; it is in France herself that, by his death, he is helping to live, and to whose salvation he has contributed. Isn't that what he wished?

27

JUSTICE OR CHARITY

IT is deplorably difficult to study the Paris newspapers in Algiers. So I could not check the accuracy of what I hear: an article of mine on "Benda's last book" must have appeared in the heroic *Combat* under the title chosen by me, in which, for greater actuality, the words *Justice* and *Charity* stand side by side, introduced by a sentence of Malebranche's quoted by Benda and which my article reproduced. This tempts me to clarify my idea on that delicate point.

Having been sworn in at the Assize Court, I no longer believe very much in Justice. (I am speaking of human justice, for, as for the divine, we shall have to wait for another life, doubtless, to meet up with it.) The disproportion between the crime and the penalty, for the crimes that one is called upon to judge to-day, remains so flagrant that one ends by understanding Lynching Law and the torture of Brinvillier. "An eye for an eye; a tooth for a tooth." But how many millions of eyes and teeth would Hitler need to be satisfied? . . . Without going any further, what relationship, what comparison between the fact of having, for so many years, poisoned public opinion in the *Action française, Je suis partout* or *Gringoire,* and confinement, even if perpetual, or death? And what is more, is it just that the poisoner should pay no more than the poisoned, and those whose sole crime will be not to have thought afterwards "as one should" ("commerce with the enemy" is often reduced to that, if at least no shameful profit was obtained by that commerce).

Justice and *Charity,* it is important that it be borne home, often do more than merely differ: they are opposed. And every haphazard compromise that tries to conciliate the two, would be a travesty of both at the same time.

* * * *

Strictly speaking, there is not a question of Justice in all the Evangels. Christians do not take sufficient notice of it. A number of them would be astonished and would protest if they heard it said that it is by that especially that the Christian religion is distinguished from all others; and on that account, it is vain to search, as is done sometimes, for a common ground of understanding between them and it. At heart, they say, we are all searching for the same thing, are we not, Catholic or Protestant Christians, Mussulmen, Jews, disciples of Confucius or of Buddha: love and peace among men, the restriction of personal feelings, the triumph of altruism, etc. . . . . That is a misunderstanding of the unique individualism of Christ's teaching, never more admirable than where it differs from all the other teachings. The idea of justice remains human. The teaching of the One who said: "Judge not" goes beyond, in a superhuman way (and the believers will say: divinely), justice. What more shocking in respect to justice than the same pay to a worker of the last hour as to the diligent worker? Than the concern for the one lost sheep taking precedence over the attention given to the rest of the flock? Than that preference of the individual to the masses? Than that disconcerting advice not to pull up the weeds, but to let them grow along with the good grain? Than that passport accorded the repentent sinner, before those who practiced good works all their lives? Than that tearing away, through love, from all other obligations considered sacred before? . . .

Is not that what makes of Christianity that remarkable school of individualism, with which it will fertilize the world? It has already been remarked how favorable for revolutions lands first worked by Christianity prove themselves to be. Would not ignoring or denying this peculiarity take away from

Christianity its most singular virtue, take the savor from the salt?

The Christian ideal defies all human prudence. Moreover it does not appear in place at a time when, to turn the left cheek after a slap received on the right, a proceeding contrary to the discipline of armies and to what we call honor, would risk bringing frightful loss on the party, on the homeland, and on all that attaches us to it. All that will be spoken of to-morrow, after victory and peace. But that is what tries certain Christian consciences so sorely, when to-day it is a question of sanctions, purging, and of giving precedence, for what may be a long time, to the entirely human and approximate idea of justice, over the one, so clearly superior, but ruinous, of charity.

28

COURAGE

THE use of the most expressive words, their best place in the sentence, its flow, balance, rhythm, harmony . . . yes, all that is a part of "good writing" (and none of it is worth while if it is not natural).

A quantity of words one uses commonly are convenient to use, as long as one does not know any too well what they mean. Everything, in our time, conspires to devaluate that fiduciary coinage that some use in a topsy-turvy way, that others abuse consciously, ready to benefit by the demoralization that results from it. The word "courage" is one of them.

Courage is measured by what one risks; and one calls dare-devils exactly those who risk very little, having practically nothing to lose and all to gain. Most of the time courage gets along without reflection. It is a sudden carrying away of a generous soul puffed up and warmed by enthusiasm, indignation, wrath; the carrying away either by hate or love almost indifferently.

Courage with a refreshed mind and a cool heart is far more meritorious (but what does the merit matter when it is a question of results?). In this, as almost everywhere, the social point of view is opposed to the individual point of view. Here I am concerned only with the latter. So much the worse. "The only courage I respect," said (so they say) Napoleon, "is that of three o'clock in the morning." That is to say: courage *on an empty stomach.* Calm balancing of the end to be obtained and the risk to be run: twofold consideration of

What I risk and what I am after.

as Corneille's Emilie said, (inexhaustible teaching of our classics! I shall never stop wondering, as a reasonable being, at the beginning of *Cinna,* so perfectly artful and so little artificial; triumph of reason over passion and instinct; triumph of man over nature, over his nature; triumph of the individual).

Sometimes I have been congratulated on my courage, when I knew and felt myself not brave at all: when what I risked was worth nothing to me, so that losing it was of no importance. And I think that the lack of courage, that I deplore among some, comes from their illusions on the real value of spurious riches, spurious honors and spurious goods. What have I to do with the respect of people I do not respect? I get along easily without it. Less easily when it is a question of friends, of those whose judgment is important to me and on which I set my heart. Sometimes, nevertheless, it has to be risked, if one insists before everything in remaining true to oneself. Come now! Let's have no misunderstanding. As for respect due to pretense, I don't want anything to do with it. You will never despise me as much as I despise falsehood. I have great concern for the respect of friendship, but let it not go with a false appearance, with a mask. I am concerned with genuine beings, others and myself; and of connections without trickery.

As for physical courage, I admire it all the more because I do not know whether I am capable of it or not. The man who resists torture, rather than betray a cause by revealing the names of accomplices, deserves the martyr's palm as much as the greatest saints. The latter at least can hope for a celestial reward; the former nothing. And whatever Pascal may say (Oh! very imprudently), death, the shedding of blood, sufferings endured, none of all that can prove the truth of what one dies or suffers for, nor the number of martyrs, for there are martyrs for every cause, for every conviction, even the worst. There are even great chances. . . . But I stop on the threshold of what might appear blasphemy. I mean only that the martyrdom of Galileo was not necessary to make the earth revolve; it is not a question of Faith; while, by their devotion, the first Christians witnessed a belief in something incredible; forcing the admission of the inadmissible.

But here now: You don't wish to admit that the earth revolves? . . . Let it be as you claim. The "Testis esto" is not out of place in face of what anyone at all is in the act of verifying. *Eppur, si muove!* . . . and you can do nothing about it. The conviction of the martyrs can do nothing in favor of the truth; but this proves at least that the Spirit is stronger than the brutality which crushes it. There is something in that which does not convince me, but astounds me. As for the martyr . . . laic, if I may say so, the most admirable, in my opinion, is the one whom no god approves, sustains or rewards, even with hope.

I have let my thoughts run on; they have carried me very far from what I had intended to say at first; and which is simply this:

When I published my first book on the Soviet Union, I was perfectly conscious that I was going to stir up protestation and hatred around me. Perfectly conscious too when, recently, I did not think I should delete pages from my *Journal* that betrayed my first depression at the time of the invasion of France. I knew they would be used against me. It certainly required no courage to write them; it did, perhaps, to publish them at a time when they could do me the most harm. But a diary which permits of touching up and tries to color the past loses its interest, its reason for existence. Not what he would have liked to be, but what he really was, is important.[1] Besides I had the right to hope that those pages would temper the fury of the accusations made against the Gionos, Jouhaudeaux, the Montherlants, against those who were deceived. That mistake of judgment was mine, too. I could be reproached as they were; I gave proof of it. If you condemn them, condemn me in the same way. But to my way of thinking, guilt begins only where the error is profitable. And that is why "capitalizable" opinions, as they say to-day, are questionable to me. That word is jargon, perhaps, but it is clear and says exactly what it means. Let us not cease to love the truth even when it is unfavorable to us.

---

1 On reading Renan's writings concerning the war of '70, I find out he fell into the same errors, and in almost exactly the same way; with, perhaps, less excuse than I, for he was much younger and better informed than I could be. But I do not write this to excuse myself.

29

TRUTH

AT the word Truth alone, ideas spring up and crowd around, like the shades on the bank of the Cocytus, imploring Charon, who is helping them to cross the river, to receive them. Which should be taken first into that navicula of words which saves them from being forgotten for a time? They jostle each other so much that I give up all priority and take them out of order.

My friend Strohl observed that the recruitment of great naturalists and observers of the phenomenal world was made much more easily among Protestants than among Catholics. That has to be verified, but would scarcely surprise me; for I have already noted how often that sort of presbyopia brought about by fixed attention on distant clarities and the contemplation of the intangible renders the aspect of the real world indifferent or insensible. Those dazzled souls are at the same time unconcerned and incapable of observing. They live in a sort of mystical phantasmagoria. . . . It goes without saying there are exceptions, and I refuse to generalize excessively; but when I heard Bauman, in his *Trois Villes Saintes,* speak of the "hairy leaves" of the cabbage, I thought irresistibly that the Virgin would not have much trouble in appearing to him. I don't think my quip attracted much notice; yet I consider it had a certain importance. Yes, I believe that it constitutes the point of departure between two kinds of truths, and that the minds most sensitive to one, to conventional truths, may very well be insensible to others, the verifiable truths. There are also truths of an historical nature. Furthermore belief, Faith, does not tempt one to research, even if it does not consider all research as challenging to authority and impious.

Reflecting well on the matter, nothing is more precarious, more fragile than this idea of the *Truth* that we too easily consider natural and, if I may say so, innate. Entire peoples, and not only primitive populations, have been able to get along very well (or very badly) without it. The same with children. They like to live in the imaginary and have no imperative concern with what is. To what degree this notion of the truth (which is by no means spontaneous) comes to be perverted in them by the pleasing tales of Santa Claus, guardian angels, the Holy Virgin, little Jesus, etc. . . . have parents no conception? and that the child, afterwards, on reaching maturity, may very well, when he takes it upon himself to cleanse his mind a bit, "throw out the child with the bath-water," as the German proverb expresses it excellently.

Upon what then is that notion of the truth to be established?

I think a number of minds do not have it naturally, get along happily without it, and even cannot understand that, in certain others, the love of truth, the need of truth, is an exigency that can take precedence over all considerations of prudence or advantageous opportunity. And I believe that Catholics, essentially and by their very formation, concerned above everything with a dogmatic and mystical truth, attach much less importance to the truths I spoke of: the verifiable ones, and I understand by that, those of the Natural Sciences and History. That could be verified at the time of the Dreyfus Affair, which cut France in half: the one for the revision of the case comprising an enormous majority of Protestants and Jews; the Catholics ranging themselves for the greater part on the side of the accepted thing and of the "let us not go back to it."

The truth, in our day, finds few defenders. Falsehood triumphs everywhere. My first, my principal grievance against Barrès, is his having aided powerfully in balancing, in young minds, that swaying notion, enthroning in its place a convenient and yielding use of a relative truth, modifiable according to circumstances and places. There were, he taught, French truths, Lorrainese truths; the true one was the opportune one.

No need to glide along far to arrive at the "equivalent truths" that a young communist explained to me as being so convenient and even indispensable to use. It is a question of getting rid of an undesirable, but of getting rid of him according to Justice, that is to say in keeping the Law on one's side. Now the crime committed is of an ideological nature so subtle that the people could not understand. For the use of the masses one can and must erect in place of the ideological subtility some great common crime susceptible of exciting indignation against that "enemy of the people," so that the people remain convinced that it is their interests that are involved and that Justice defends.

Useless to insist, comrade; I have understood; you have the power: so you must be right. . . . .

30

TWO IMAGINARY INTERVIEWS

I

THE Interviewer.—In its fight against Naturalism, or Realism, we recognize, dear Master, that art, that literature at least, at the time of your *Nourritures terrestres,* with its tendency toward the artificial, smelled terribly musty. But, without going back to it, let us pass on. I should like, I was telling you, to make one criticism of your introduction[1], which appears to me important. It seems, if I understand you (and I am thinking particularly of some sentences in your conclusion), it seems, I say, as though man were forced to choose between the Christian position and that taken by Goethe. As though there were not many ways to escape the hold of Christianity without joining Goethe!

I.—I do not say . . .

He.—And in the first place, when you speak of

[1] It concerns the *Introduction to the Theatre of Goethe,* which had just appeared in *The Figaro* during the spring of 1942.

the "help of Grace," I think you embody in those words all supernatural intervention, every appeal to any religion whatever. But, even then, man has many ways of exerting himself without going over to Goethe and the field remains clear . . .

I.—Nevertheless, the examples I quote, of Nietzsche, Leopoldi and Hoelderlin (and I could have quoted many others) should leave no doubt as to my idea. Goethe does not teach heroism, and we need heroes. Christianity can lead us into heroism, of which one of the finest forms is saintliness; but every hero is not necessarily a Christian.

He.—Nor every Christian a hero! Heaven only knows! I know only too many, and you too, who are beyond the pale.

I.—Free thinking does not always retain the indulgent smile of Renan, the sarcasm of Voltaire, or the detachment of France. The non-acquiescence to dogmas and simple integrity of mind has been able to lead many to martyrdom. A martyr without palms, without hope of reward and, for this reason, all the more admirable. Without going that far, let us say that human dignity, and that sort of moral bearing, of "consistency" to which we attach all our hopes to-day, gets along very well without the support and comfort of the Faith. In these recent times, Christians have given fine examples, both Protestants and Catholics, before which we have only to bow our heads; but I hold it a very grave error to think, with a great number of fine minds, that France must and can find her salvation only in attachment to a Credo.

When a ship is in distress, those who kneel down and intone chants address prayers and supplications to the Most-High . . . that is fine; tears come into my eyes only at the thought of it. And at least they keep back the cries of the women and children, and the crazed rushing about that would disturb the maneuvers of the crew. But just the same, if the ship is to be saved, it will not be by clasped hands.

He.—Montherlant says some daring things in this respect.

I.—Which please me. And wait a minute; I see in him an excellent example of anti-Christianity not like Goethe's.

He.—You would like from him, don't you agree, parallels to the *Lives of the Saints* and *The Golden Legend,* some biographies that would, in themselves, have nothing *legendary* about them, which he would write so well! valorous heroes, entirely human, according to his taste (and yours doubtless); among others, the Marshal Strozzi, cousin to Catherine di Medicis.

I.—I remember only in what special esteem he was held by Montaigne who admired in him, at the same time, the warrior of great merit in his "military competence" and the scholar; a very fine passage in the *Essays* congratulates him on having chosen Caesar's *Commentaries* for bedside reading. "They should be," he said, "the breviary of every military man."

He.—What Montaigne does not tell us and that Brantôme told, is that Strozzi, as learned in Greek as in Latin, had translated Caesar into the Greek language with "Latin annotations, the finest additions and instructions for soldiers," says Brantôme, "that I ever saw or that were ever written."

I.—That should delight Montherlant, indeed.

He.—The account of his death is of a nature especially likely to please him, such as we read it in Vieilleville's *Mémoires*. When Strozzi was mortally wounded by a musket shot at the siege of Thionville, on June 20, 1558, the Duke de Guise went to him, Vieilleville tells us, exhorting him to repentance. But you must read the text itself: I copied it; one would hate to change or lose a single word. Listen. He took a note-book from his pocket and read to me:

Then the Duke de Guise, "recalling the name of Jesus:—'What Jesus, for heaven's sake,' said Strozzi, 'are you trying to bring to me? I deny God. My good times are over.' And the prince redoubling his pleas told him that he should think of God and that that very day he would be face to face with Him. 'Heavens!' he responded, 'I shall be where all the others are who have been dead for six thousand years'."

I.—Six thousand years! . . . To-day we know that is an understatement.

He.—Wait a minute! Wait a minute! And Vieilleville adds, in his charming manner, don't you agree? "Everything is in the Italian language."

I.—I recognize that this ending does not lack grandeur. It is almost as difficult, if not more so, to die well as to live well. But then Strozzi had neither wife nor family with him. Ah! I understand Montaigne's wishing to die far away from his people, a death all his own, not distorted by pity or sympathy. . . . It is an article of death that one expects from the great souls under discussion. In the death struggle they relax, let themselves go to the priest who is lying in wait, with the aid of a wife's objurgations, or a sister's, or a mother's. Then the Church is quick to take possession of their past and of their very resistance which at first they had opposed to it.

He.—Yet you admit . . .

I.—Why yes; I admit all the rest. I give in; I acquiesce, and even, as well as I can, I understand . . .

He.—It concerns the salvation of souls. Put yourself at their point of view.

I.—That's all I do, I roared, put myself at other people's point of view. I've done nothing else all my life; to such a degree that it is my own point of view which becomes difficult for me to find again later. And yet that is the important thing. To depend constantly on others in order to judge, form an opinion, is to take the savor from the salt.

He.—"And if the salt loses its savor, with what shall it be salted?" Yes, I know you have been nourished on the gospels. You come back to them in spite of yourself.

I.—Now you annoy me. It is true: I feel you there, on the scent of some sentence that may compromise me. . . . Mind your own business and simply do your duty as an interviewer. If you try again to make me talk more than I intend to, I shall slam the door in your face. Consider that final. . . .

Come now! Sit down again. But let us go back to literature. May I ask you in my turn, if during the long time that I have left you, you have progressed in your book.

He.—To tell the truth, no. But it is mellowing. What bothers me is that I should like to say nothing in it that is not essential, general, universal.

I.—But my dear friend, be sure to tell yourself that, in art, nothing general is attained except through the particular. That is what Goethe understood so well.

He.—Haven't you anything more to say to me about him?

I.—Not to-day at least. You have worn me out. Come back.

II

I.—I let myself be carried away ridiculously the other day; I beg you to excuse me. Immediately after your departure, reflecting on what had put me out, I thought that . . .

He.—Allow me: it is you who are coming back to it. However you promised to touch on nothing with me again except literary questions.

I.—But on certain days you stifle at always hiding what fills up your heart.

He.—You were then thinking that . . . you were saying?

I.—That what upsets and holds me back is certainly not the Gospels, which contain better advice than any other book in the world. And I was even forced to understand very quickly that what I was looking for formerly in communism (in vain, for where I hoped to find love, I found only theory), was what Christ teaches us, teaches us with all the rest additional.

He.—Then, what stops you?

I.—It is that act of blind credulity the Church requires: Faith. Reason itself, with love, leads me to the Gospels; so why deny reason?

He.—Does the Faith deny it?

I.—Good heavens, yes; that is, strictly speaking, what makes up "believing." One believes contrary to all verification, to all evidence. In order to "believe" you have to put out your eyes. The object of belief, to stop looking at it in order to see it. You know very well that belief in a personal God, in Providence, implies abdication of everything reasonable in us. I even prefer, and very much so, the *Quia absurdum* to every rational effort of some to attach to a divine plan the dangerous effects of forces and natural laws, or the criminal follies of mankind. It is franker and more honest, and the believer has won the game as soon as he refuses to play it. Won for himself at least. For, as for me, to believe in that God he proposes to me would lead me very quickly into saying with Orestes:

In whatever direction I turn my eyes,
I see only misfortunes that condemn that God.

I find more consolation in considering God as an invention, a creation of man, that man composes little by little, tends to form more and more, by means of his intelligence and virtue. It is in Him that creation has its end, its aim, and not from Him that it emanates. And as time does not exist for the Eternal, that amounts to the same thing, for Him.

He.—It seems to me Renan said just about that.

I.—Oh! don't interrupt me, I beg you! I have enough trouble already following my thoughts . . . Where was I? . . . Oh, yes. Faith. And notice that for them, the believers, nothing but that counts. A life devoted to search for the truth is nothing, for the only truth, for them, is that Truth that one "would not search for if one had not already found it." And that Truth, all found, is sufficient for everything, suffices to cover every life of dissipation and error.

He.—It is true also that belief in that Truth brings about a betterment in the life.

I.—Or at least should bring it about. But what is the use of quibbling about it? The very property of dogma is to be indisputable. So let's not dispute it.

He.—And yet you admit the teaching of the Gospels.

I.—With all my heart, yes; but outside of (apart from) Faith. Now, if I should put every teaching of Christ into practice, conform my life to it, in the eyes of the believer, none of all that would count without Faith.

He.—You are wrong. All that retains its importance. I fear you have been misinformed. You are judging from your old memories. The Church of to-day shows itself ready to recognize, even in unbelievers, good habits and good will, every effort toward the good and the true. Deploring only that these efforts are not offered to the Lord, the Church to-day is much more disposed to pity than to condemn.

I.—Why yes; I am not ignorant of the fact that the Church has very charitably and wisely withdrawn its frontal attack. It would no longer condemn Galileo, good heavens! It does not stop, nor will it stop in its progress backwards. *L'Histoire Universelle* of Bossuet makes even priests smile to-day. Step by step, the Church is losing ground, beats a retreat, yields. . . .

He.—And in this withdrawal orthodoxy is strengthened.

I.—My mind refuses to submit itself to any orthodoxy whatever.

He.—And yet you recognize the excellency of the Gospel precepts. Their finest putting in practice loses all meaning without Faith.

I.—Say that they take on a different one, and one for which I have a preference.

He.—Yes, through pride.

I.—I was expecting that word. Believers owe it to themselves to give a disparaging interpretation to everything great and noble and fine in independence.

He.—Independence! Ah! the time has come to talk about it! Yet you recognize that to-day it is important to group, organize, bring under the yoke in order to employ, to subject, to make useful. . . .

I.—Finish it; say, to administer the oath. . . . One can always find excellent motives for repudiating reason and keeping man from thinking. Unite wills, that's all very well; nothing great is accomplished without submission and discipline. But, through a forced devotion, to prevent reason from exercising itself, to regulate thought on order, that can lead only to a general stupefying. *Amissa virtute pariter ac libertate,* with no one left to be aware of it, no one to suffer from it; for inactivity of the mind is like that of the body, and every other form of sloth; first one accepts grumblingly, then the mind quickly takes its ease in an outwardly devotional acquiescence, and that's just where the danger lies; *Invisa primo desidia, postremo amatur.*

He.—What in the world has gotten you to quoting so much Latin?

I.—That's because, for the past few days, I have been buried in Tacitus.

He.—Do you read him easily?

I.—More easily than I would have thought; but not without a translation on the opposite page, and with inexpressible satisfaction. Without doubt I am delighted with the impulsive manner of a Stendhal, whose idea one seems always to be surprising on getting out of bed, before making one's toilet. I do not like thoughts which are made up and decked out, but those that are concentrated and compact. Tacitus' sentence is taut. It is his *Life of Agricola* that I am reading, and from the beginning I was conquered. What authority! What gravity! What fervor! How pleased I am, more than by ease or grace, with that austere, savage asperity! I take this book with me; I read as I walk; I roll under my tongue without exhausting all the bitter sap, some of the vigorous sentences by which my will is stiffened: "With the voice we should have lost our memory, if it had been as easy to forget as to remain silent" . . . *Si tam in nostra potestate esset oblivisci quam tacere*. What precedes it is equally fine. Reread it.

He.—You read a great deal.

I.—I have never read so much, nor so well; with a sort of eagerness as in my youth and which, when I think of my age, appears to me a little ridiculous; but I can't do anything about it; I think as little as possible about my age, and when I think of it, it is to say to myself: hurry up. But this digression carries us. . . .

He.—Not at all. It leads us back to God. Everything leads the attentive soul back to God. Why don't you recognize in the "hurry up" His Call? "Hurry up and give me your heart, love Me."

I.—I am going to try to explain myself. Not so much to explain to you as to explain to myself the point at which my thought has slowly arrived almost in spite of myself.

There can be no question of two Gods. But I take care not to confuse, under this name of God, two very different things, different to the point of opposing each other. On one hand, the whole of Cosmos and the natural laws that govern it; matter and forces, energies; that is the role of Zeus; and that can be called God, but on taking out of the word all personal meaning and morality. On the other hand, the fascicles of every human effort toward the good and the beautiful; the slow mastery of brute forces and their putting into service in order to realize the good and beautiful on earth; that is the role of Prometheus; and Christ's role, too; it is the unfolding of man, and all the virtues have part in it. But this God does not inhabit nature at all; he is created by man, or, if you prefer, it is through man that he creates himself; and every effort to exteriorize him by prayer remains futile. It was with him that Christ joined; but it is to the other one he addresses himself when, dying, he utters his despairing cry: "My God, why hast thou forsaken me? . . ."

He.—In order that "all be accomplished," says the believer.

I.—But I who do not believe see in it only a tragic misapprehension. There is no desertion there because there was never an understanding; because the god of natural forces has no ears and remains indifferent to human sufferings, either in attaching Prometheus to the Caucasus, or in nailing Christ to the cross.

He.—Allow me: it was not natural forces that crucified Christ; it was man's malignity.

I.—The God whom Christ represents and incarnates, the God-Virtue, must fight at the same time against Zeus and man's malignity. That last word of Christ (the only one of the seven words of the Crucified reported by two Evangelists, the simple apostles Matthew and Mark, who report only that word) keeps me from confusing Christ with God, if all the rest had not already warned me. How can one not see, in that tragic word, not a letting go, a treachery on God's part, but this: that Christ, believing and making others believe that he was one with God, was mistaken and deceived us; that the One he called "my Father" had never recognized him for Son, that the God he represented, that he himself, was only, as he sometimes says, "the Son of Man?" It is that God only whom I am able and wish to adore.

31

LEAVES

February 1942.

MADEMOISELLE CHARRAS, with pious and affectionate intentions, had sent me, at La Croix, during the last Easter holidays, a little book of Protestant propaganda: *For Faith, Unity and Action.* I did not open it until last evening. It contains, independent of all context, only the words of Christ, and all of Christ's words. It is a book in good faith, composed, or at least enlightened, by A. Westphal. But I find fault with a good deal of it. In the first place, his translation of the Gospel texts; I return to the reproaches I made them at the time of *Numquid et tu. . . .* His desire to touch souls leads him into bringing the words of Christ to us. Of those that do not seem to him sufficiently clear, he forces the sense slightly and twists it a little, in such a way, he believes, as to permit us to understand better; but immediately he limits its extent, and the significance loses in breadth what it gains in exactitude.

I shall hunt for no better example than the one I light on at once: Christ's word to Mary Magdalene after the resurrection, that *Noli me tangere,* which is addressed in turn to every loving soul and anticipates every mystical aspiration,—for the words become, according to Westphal: "Don't attach yourself to me, for . . ." And naturally that is very easily understood: Mary Magdalene should not attach herself to the Christ so as not to disturb and hinder the Christ who must ascend to the Father. That is reasonable and brief. Those words lose their infinite reverberation.

But this bothers me still more:

Of Christ's seven words on the cross, three are reported to us by Luke:

1—*Father, forgive them for they know not what they do.*

2—*To-day shalt thou be with me in Paradise* (word spoken to the one called "the good thief").

3—*Father, into thy hands I commend my spirit.*

Three are handed down to us by John:

1—*Woman, behold thy son* (to the Virgin Mary) and *Behold thy mother* (to the one of the disciples "whom Jesus loved").

2—*I thirst.*

3—*It is finished.*

For those six solemn words, loaded with inexhaustible meaning, no "concordance." The seventh is the only one handed down to us, at the same time, by two Evangelists, who bring us only that one. I say "the seventh," but merely because I am quoting it last. It is important to notice that it has been handed down to us by the two of the four Evangelists, by far the most simple and the least concerned with doctrine and mystical interpretation. They report only this one word, and both of them give it as the last one of Christ; and this word is terrible; it is the tragic cry of every soul that puts its confidence in a God that does not exist. Or, without going so far, for it in no way denies the existence of God, at least it disassociates God from Christ, opposes them (as I do irresistibly): *My God! My God! why have you forsaken me?*

In that word alone, how can one help seeing, shockingly, not a letting go, a betrayal on the part of God, but this: that Christ, believing and making others believe that he was a part of God, was mistaken and misled us; that the one he called "his Father" had never recognized him for "Son" and that all the superhuman teaching of Christ took place outside of God, even in opposition to him.

Naturally Westphal takes care not to give this cry of despair as the last word of Christ. It is important for the believer to be reassured, and for that reason, to join it to *I thirst.* So it takes on the meaning of a temporary and quasi-human weakness in which Christ suffers and doubts in as much as he is man and "the word made flesh." And this word must be followed immediately by the *It is finished,* by which the mission of Christ is confirmed, as he assumes, in view of saving humanity, every weakness and suffering that belongs to man. Then, finally, in order to establish the sonship firmly: *Father, into thy hands I commend my spirit.*

The terrible word can be explained in the following manner: Momentary weakness, for "the flesh is weak," and in this very weakness is the proof that Jesus was really made man, consenting to suffer in human flesh. And God, although He is love, refuses to help him, in order that "everything be accomplished." The frightful sacrifice must be accepted to the end. "Why have you abandoned me?" So that humanity might be saved through you. Otherwise you would not be the Savior.

Thus everything becomes clear, logical and reassuring. But that is not at all the way it has been presented to us. Luke and John, much more sentient than Mark and Matthew, bring to their account a concern that goes way beyond that of the simple chroniclers and reporters that the first two guileless Evangelists are. Luke and John do not even report a word that appears to them, as it is, very dangerous.

I come across the rough copy of a letter that I addressed to Mademoiselle M.S. Saint-Cyr on August 15, 1941, in answer to a letter I had just received from her. It is not out of place for me to transcribe it in this notebook:

"Every effort by man to build up virtue capable of triumphing over brute force, effort that found its highest representative in the Christ, is opposed to that totality of natural laws in which I can recognize no providential intervention. The "Eli Eli Lama Sabachtani" of the Christ, that desperate, despairing cry, could be uttered by all of us without ceasing, as soon as we try to find a God anywhere else than in the moral domain. The mesalliance that the Catholics try to establish between a god, master of nature and a god-providence (or simply a god realized humanly in the Christ) appears to me cause for misunderstanding between you and me. Those two worlds, the physical and the moral, remain in constant antagonism. I can not believe in two gods.

"I can recognize none of the attributes likely to make God worthy of adoration (but only of fear) in the physical world on which our bodies depend and whose laws are immutable. Nevertheless, our most praiseworthy effort is to master it by science and the knowledge of those laws, and then to apply that knowledge to a more and more efficacious exercise of increasingly generous virtues. I am willing to call God the fascicles of those virtues invented by man and that love which radiates from the Gospels; but then that is only to raise him up with all my human strength against that Zeus, against that pitiless and mechanical totality of the laws that govern our universe. Otherwise, if my mind assimilates God into those laws, it is only to come up unfailingly against fearful contradictions, against the unthinkable.

"The constant drama of humanity is the one played between Prometheus and Zeus, between mind and matter, between love and brute force, between Christ and the indifference of Heaven; drama of which a new act is unfolding at present; drama in which we neither can nor should remain non-participating witnesses, and which, for victory against Zeus, requires from us "the strength of lions and the wisdom of serpents."

"Do not make me regret having said so much to you, I beg you. The confidence in your letter invited me to do so. With my very deepest regards, Mademoiselle, believe me. . . ."

Yes, I know that the drop of water carried along by its weight, can ascend to the sky in vapor only to fall again in rain. But the wear and tear of rock, the gravel that the stream carries to the river and the river to the sea, the granite that disintegrates, I know that all that will not again go up the fatal incline; and the highest mountains dissolve into the valley, the plain where their ruins accumulate and become equal. Everything falls from a height less and less lofty with a fall more and more shallow. This inevitable leveling is accomplished hour by hour and minute by minute under our very eyes. In like manner the whole material world equalizes and tempers its energies. I was still young when that idea began to haunt me, an idea which I now find expressed scientifically and which is not, therefore, absurd.

I should like to offer as a counterbalance to it, that other idea which has itself escaped science: that this leveling of matter has a corresponding progressive variation in the mind.

"No one comes to the Father (to God), except through me." To begin with God himself. It is through Christ that God is made.

. . . so that at last
It all amounts to this—the sovereign proof
That we devote ourselves to God, is seen
In living just as though no God there were.
(BROWNING. *Paracelsus!*)

The mind advances only over the dead bodies of ideas. To-day it is no longer possible to think what yesterday one considered certain: that the earth is flat; that the sun turns about it; that nature abhors a vacuum; and, more recently, that the atom is indecomposable etc.; the same thing on the mystical plane, although with many more laggards. A number of minds, and some of the best, still believe in Providence. It seems to them that all would be lost if the rock on which the believer has firmly placed his foot, and that he has believed firm, should totter. To move the foundation to a neighboring rock, firm until, in its turn, it totters, is, strictly speaking, progress.

I can not believe in the immortality of the soul without, at the same time, believing in metempsychosis. In order not to be obliged to come to an end . . . it is necessary never to have begun. I do not even understand how believers can be unembarrassed where my thought stumbles, and prolonging life beyond death, do not immediately feel the need to prolong it equally before birth.

32

AUTUMN LEAVES

Neuchâtel, November 1947.

I SHALL be able to say "amen" to anything whatever that happens to me, even if it means to exist no longer, to disappear after having existed. But now I exist and do not understand any too well what that means. I should like to see the matter clearly.

For pity's sake, leave me alone. I need a little silence around me to obtain peace within myself.

How troublesome you are! . . . I need to meditate.

"Free-thinking" . . . X. explains to me that true liberty of thought must be sought on the side of the believer, not on mine.

"For," he reasoned, "your mind is held on leash by logic."

I agreed that a remarkable freedom of thought was necessary to believe in the miracles and all that follows; and that I saw very well that his own mind did not revolt against admitting what to me (and to him) appeared contrary to reason. That is even the property of Faith. Where you can not verify or prove, you must *believe.*

"And if you refuse to believe," he concluded, "stop telling me and claiming that you love liberty."

In my heart, I knew very well that I was not a "free-thinker."

Faith can remove mountains; yes, mountains of absurdities[1]. To Faith, I do not oppose doubt, but the affirmation: what could not be, is not.

Therefore I shall refuse to consider the finality in nature. According to the best advice, I shall everywhere replace systematically the *why* by the *how.* For instance, I know (or at least I have been told) that the substance which the silkworm discharges in forming his cocoon, would poison him if he kept it in him. He expurgates it. It is for his salvation that he empties himself. Which does not prevent the cocoon, which he is obliged to form under penalty of death, and which he would not know how and would be unable to form differently, from protecting the metamorphosis of the caterpillar; and that the latter can only become a butterfly when empty of this silky poison. . . . But at the same time, I am forced to wonder at the degree to which the *how* here joins the *why,* unites with it so closely, cleaves to it so tightly that I can not distinguish one from the other.

---

1 See *in fine.*

It is the same thing for the mollusk and the shell. The same thing everywhere incessantly; in nature, the solution is not separate from the problem. Or better expressed: there is no problem; there are only solutions. Man's mind invents the problem afterwards. He sees problems everywhere. It's a scream.[1]

Ah! if my mind would only drop its dead ideas as a tree its faded leaves! And without too many regrets, if it is possible! Those from which the sap has receded. But in heaven's name! What beautiful colors!

Those ideas which you think at first you can not do without. From that the great danger of establishing one's moral comfort on false ideas. Let us examine, let us verify first. Formerly the sun turned around the earth; the latter, a fixed point, remained the center of the world, God's center of attention. . . And then, not at all! It is the earth that revolves. But then everything is tottering! Everything is lost! . . . Nevertheless nothing is changed but the belief. Man must learn to get along without it. He frees himself first from one, then from the other. To get along without Providence: man is weaned.

We are not there yet. That state of complete atheism requires considerable virtue to attain; and even more to maintain. The "believer" will see in it

---

[1] This is the first time I use that terrible word, the only one that fits.

doubtless only an invitation to license. If it were so: long live God! Long live the sacred lie that would preserve mankind from bankruptcy, from disaster. But can not man learn to require from himself by virtue what he thinks required by God? Nevertheless he will have to come to that; some at least, at first; without it, the game would be lost. It will only be won, this strange game we are playing here upon earth (without wanting to, without knowing it, and often against our inclination) if it is to virtue that the idea of God gives place as it recedes; if it is man's virtue, his dignity, that replaces and supplants God. God exists only by virtue of man. *Et eritis sicut dei* (That is how I wish to understand that old word of the Tempter—who, like God, exists only in our minds—and see in that offer, that we have been told is fallacious, a possibility of salvation).

God is virtue. But what do I mean by that? It must be defined; I do not succeed very well. I shall only succeed later. But I shall already have done a great deal if I remove God from the altar and put man in his place. Temporarily I think that virtue is the highest an individual can obtain from himself.

God will come later. I persuade myself and repeat constantly: it depends on us. It is through us that God is realized.

What rubbish all this literature is! And even if I should consider only the most successful writings, what business have I, when life is there, with those reflections, those duplicates of life! The only thing that matters to me is what can lead me to modify my way of seeing and acting. To live, all my courage is not too much; to live in this frightful world. . . . And I know and feel that it is frightful; but I know also that it would be possible for it not to be so, and that it is what we make it. If you denounce the present horror of it, to bring a protest by indignation or disgust, bravo! But if not, away with demoralizers!

There could very well have been nothing; nor anybody. Nobody to notice that there was nothing, and to find that natural.

But what a strange thing that there is something, anything at all.

Something and not a void. Century upon century was necessary to produce this something, to free this something or other from chaos. Still more centuries to obtain the least life. And again still more for this life to reach consciousness. I have ceased to understand, and from its very beginning, this advance, this history. But more incomprehensible than all the rest: unselfishness. Let people go into ecstasies, wrongly without doubt, before the maternal or conjugal abnegation, or altruistical, of the animals; it can be explained, reduced; properly speaking there is nothing disinterested in it; everything follows its inclination and pleasure. I grant it; but it is to wonder all the more when I find these sublime sentiments in man, and capable of gratuitousness. I bend the knee before the slightest act of abnegation, of self-sacrifice for another, for an abstract duty, for an idea. If that is to be the end, the whole world is not too much, all the immense misery of mankind.

They do not admit serenity acquired outside of what they teach. I speak here of the Catholics; every doctrine that departs from their church must end in despair.

As for that serenity on which you plume yourself, you expose it by speaking of it; by exposing it, you compromise it. It is on your countenance and in your acts that one should read it; not in the sentences that you write not knowing why nor for whom. . . .

Get along without God. . . . I mean: get along without the idea of God, the belief in an attentive Providence, tutelary and rewarding . . . all who wish it, do not succeed.

Yet the bat with sunken eyes is able to avoid the wires strung up in the room where he is flying about without colliding with them. And he doubtless feels afar off, in the nocturnal air, the passing of some insect which will furnish his nourishment. He does not fly haphazardly, and his bearing which appears capricious to us, is motivated. Space is full of vibrations, rays, that our senses can not perceive, but which are intercepted by the antennae of insects. What connection between our sensations and their cause? Without a sensitive receiver, nature remains mute, colorless and odorless. It is within us that number becomes harmony.

The wonder is that man has been able to fabricate instruments capable of supplying the insufficiency of his senses, of picking up imperceptible waves and unheard vibrations. We were already satisfied with our senses; the rest is superfluous. But whether we wish it or not, the rest is there. Man has daringly widened his reception and unlimited his power. Too bad he does not show himself more equal to it! He bears himself ill. Lack of habit, perhaps (let us hope so) ; all of that is so new! He is trespassing and he is overwhelmed.

When I learned that little knots of ribbon were called rosettes (how old could I have been? Five or six . . .) I got a quantity of both of them from my mother's workbox, then, having locked myself in my room, away from looks that would have disturbed the miracle, I arranged a flower-bed, a whole garden, on the floor. Were they not flowers? The word meant that. It was only necessary to believe. And I tried for a good quarter of an hour. Nothing happened.

On a childish plane, that was the defeat of nominalism. And perhaps, after all, I lacked imagination.

But I especially remember saying to myself: "What an idiot I am. What does all this foolishness mean? There is nothing there but pieces of ribbon, nothing at all . . ." and I went and put them back in my mother's basket.

These are such hard times, that we can not imagine (or rather: are not willing to admit) that there could have been just as tragic ones at any other moment in history. Better informed, we should arrive, perhaps, at convincing ourselves that the exceptional was, very much to the contrary, the long period of tolerance in which we were living before the breaking out of horrors (which feel themselves decidedly *at home*—on earth)—so natural did that freedom of mind, so deplorably compromised to-day, appear to us. Here comes back a time when those will be considered traitors who do not think "properly."

Some, it is true, still resist; and it is they alone who count. It is of little importance that they are few in number: it is in them that the idea of God takes refuge.

But the temptation which, for the young, is the most difficult to resist, is that of "enlisting," as is said. Everything tempts one to it, the most skillful sophisms, motives the most noble in appearance and the most urgent. Much would have been accomplished if youth were persuaded that, at heart, it is through laisser-aller and laziness that they enlist;

. . . if youth were persuaded that it is a question—not of being this or that but—of being.

One flatters oneself, or at least one has the tendency to flatter oneself. Complacency toward oneself is a trap into which I have such great fear of falling that I have often been able to doubt the sincerity (the genuineness) of movements, that were, nevertheless, natural to me, as soon as they took the direction that I would have liked them to take. (My sentence is frightfully complicated; impossible to express that simply.) Those movements, those "states of mind," I still had to recognize and admit as natural, when I found them exactly the same, in my daughter while still a child; in particular, a certain fundamental optimism, that, in myself, I could be afraid was *obtained.*

As someone asked Catherine, a little stupidly, it seems to me: "Where would you rather be? At Saint-Clair (where she was then) or in Paris?"—at first she seemed very much astonished; she could scarcely comprehend that such a question deserved asking; then ended by answering ingenuously:—"why, at Saint-Clair, *since I am there.*" (She must have been hardly more than five years old at that time.) And I suddenly recognized in her the very depths of my own nature and the secret of my happiness: an "Amen" indicated by the great difficulty, if not the impossibility (in that child as in myself) of producing and nourishing regrets.

To take things as they are.
Play with the cards one has.
Require one to be what one is.

Which does not keep me from fighting against all lies, falsifications etc. brought about by man and imposed on natural things against which it is vain to revolt. There is the inevitable and the modifiable. The acceptance of the modifiable is by no means included in the *Amor Fati.*

Which does not prevent one either from requiring the best from oneself, after one has recognized it as such. For one does not make a better *likeness* of oneself by giving way to the less good.

P.S. When I brought out these pages to-day, it seemed to me that I was wrong to tear up the first ones in this notebook. As bad as they were (I had just gotten up after an illness) they answered in advance remarks made to me by a friend, in whose wisdom I have great confidence; he never speaks for the purpose of saying nothing and says only sensible things. He protests that these pages, which I have just given him to read, are much less subversive than I seemed at first to think; even that a great number of eminent representatives of the Church would willingly subscribe to them to-day; and he quotes some names that I take care not to repeat. X. and Y. were already speaking to me in the same manner, affirming that I was not very cognizant of the present state of the Church, the intelligent pliancy of its Credo. I admitted I was not at all "up to date" and that, for greater convenience doubtless, I kept to what Bossuet taught me; that as soon as it was a question of *Variations,* it could only be the *Protestant Churches* (according to the title itself of his admirable work) to which the Catholic Church was opposed, by "its character of immutability in the faith."

"Without doubt," he responded, "but nevertheless it evolves ceaselessly. You would like to harden it, to make of it a finished product; it is living and answers the new requirements. Remember Chesterton's beautiful pages, translated by Claudel, that you made me read in the *N. R. F.* some time ago? 'The Church,' he said, 'is never static'." And he compared it to a cart running at full speed over a narrow ridge avoiding new perils to right and left ceaselessly. "There is not a doubt," continues my friend, "that enlightened Catholics would not be troubled at all by the affirmations you have just stated. It is your right to call Virtue what they call God; a mere question of words; it is the same thing. The idea of God, the need for God torments you; they ask nothing more of you in order to recognize you as one of theirs. And as I nevertheless protest that there is a misunderstanding; that I am searching for what makes them reject me just the same, I return to those opening pages, written in this notebook, those badly done pages, torn up; they treated of eternal life; a sort of premonitory instinct tempted me to put them at the beginning; to speak of that first, and now I understand that it was, indeed, necessary to begin with that.

That the life of the "soul" prolongs itself beyond the dissolution of the flesh, for me, is inadmissible and unthinkable, and something against which my reason protests; as well as against the incessant expanding of souls.

BIBLIOGRAPHICAL INDEX

The following texts first appeared:

Spring, in one volume, (Flammarion) "The Garland of the Years" (texts from André Gide, Jules Romains, Colette and François Mauriac), 1941; then in the magazine *Verve,* series II, No. 5-6, p. 15.

Youth, in the *Nouvelle Revue Française,* Sept. 1931.

My Mother, in the magazine *Quatre-Vents,* Feb. 1942.

The Day of September 27, in the magazine *Commune,* Jan. 1936.

Acquasanta (with *Youth*), in a volume entitled "Two Tales," in a limited edition, 1938.

Dindiki, in the magazine *Commerce,* IX, autumn 1926.

Joseph Conrad, in the *Nouvelle Revue Française,* Dec. 1, 1924.

Francis Jammes, in the *Nouvelle Revue Française,* December 1, 1938.

The Radiance of Paul Valéry, in the daily paper *Le Figaro,* July 25, 1945.

Paul Valéry, in the magazine *l'Arche,* October 1945.

Henri Ghéon, in the weekly *Gavroche,* June 14, 1945.

Eugène Dabit, in the *Nouvelle Revue Française,* Dec. 1, 1938.

Christian Beck, in the Belgian magazine *La Nervie,* special number devoted to Christian Beck, 1931.

Antonin Artaud, in the daily *Combat,* March 19, 1948, and in the special number devoted to Antonin Artaud of the magazine *84,* 1948, No. 5-6.

Le Mercure de France, in the number 1000 of the *Mercure de France,* bearing the combined dates: July 1940 - December 1946.

La Revue Blanche, in the magazine *Labyrinthe,* 1946.

Goethe, in the Nouvelle Revue Française, March 1, 1932.

The Teaching of Poussin, as an introduction to the illustrated volume "Poussin" (edition *Au Divan*) 1945.

Lautréamont, as an introduction to the volume "The Case of Lautréamont" (*Le Disque vert,* Paris-Brussels, R. van den Berg), 1925.

Arthur Rimbaud, in the magazine *Poésie 41,* No. 6, 1941 (in answer to the inquiry: "Did Arthur Rimbaud die fifty years ago?").

Three meetings with Verlaine, in the magazine *Fontaine,* June 1942.

Literary Memories and Problems of To-day, in pamphlet form, with the *Lettres Françaises,* Beyrouth, 1946, and in *l'Arche,* No. 18-19, August-September 1946.

Preface to Night Flight, as an introduction to Saint-Exupéry's work, 1931.

Some Recent Writings of Thomas Mann, in the weekly *Marianne,* Sept. 22, 1937.

Preface for a French translation of "Morgenlandfahrt" by Hermann Hesse, "A Trip to the Orient," translated by Jean Lambert. Calman-Lévy, 1947; then in the magazine *Paru,* No. 50, January 1949.

Letter-Preface to Chants de Départ by Jean Lacaze, as an introduction to the volume (Finham, edit. *Chantal*), 1947.

Justice or Charity, in the daily *Le Figaro,* Feb. 25, 1945.

Courage, in the daily *Combat,* April 28, 1948.

Truth, in the daily *Combat,* April 29, 1948.

Two Imaginary Interviews, in the volume "Attendu que . . ." (Algiers, Edit. Charlot), 1943; in France, in *l'Arche,* No. 11, Nov. 1945.

Leaves, the first part in "Attendu que . . ." and *l'Arche,* No. 11; the second part only in the pamphlet "Two Imaginary Interviews" (Charlot), 1946.

Autumn Leaves, in the magazine *La Table Ronde,* No. 6, June 1948.

INDEX OF PROPER NAMES

INDEX

Lightning Source UK Ltd.
Milton Keynes UK
UKHW011150040322
399574UK00001B/65